TARTS AND PIES

HAMLYN
new
COOKERY

TARTS AND PIES

MARY CADOGAN

First published in Great Britain in 1994
by Hamlyn
an imprint of Reed Consumer Books Limited
Michelin House, 81 Fulham Road, London SW3 6RB
and Auckland, Melbourne, Singapore and Toronto

ISBN 0 600 58080 6

A CIP catalogue record for this book is available from the
British Library

Printed in the UK by Butler and Tanner

ACKNOWLEDGEMENTS

Art Director Jacqui Small
Art Editor Meryl James
Designer Barbara Zuniga
Commissioning Editor Nicky Hill
Copy editor Jeni Fleetwood
Editorial Assistant Kathy Steer
Production Controller Sasha Judelson
Photographer Roger Stowell
Step-by-step Photography Jonathan Lovekin
Home Economist Maxine Clark
Stylist Helen Payne

For Austin and Finbar

NOTES

Both metric and imperial measurements have been given
in all recipes. Use one set of measurements only and not a
mixture of both.

Standard level spoon measurements are used in all recipes.
1 tablespoon = one 15 ml spoon
1 teaspoon = one 5 ml spoon

Eggs should be size 3 unless otherwise stated.

Milk should be full fat unless otherwise stated.

Pepper should be freshly ground black pepper unless
otherwise stated.

Fresh herbs should be used unless otherwise stated. If
unavailable use dried herbs as an alternative but halve
the quantities stated.

Ovens should be preheated to the specified temperature
- if using a fan assisted oven, follow the manufacturer's
instructions for adjusting the time and the temperature.

CONTENTS

INTRODUCTION

I have always enjoyed making pastry. Ever since I was a young girl making the apple pie for Sunday lunch, I have found something incredibly satisfying about the task. It's not just the feel of the pastry between your fingers, or the wonderful smell of baking wafting through the house. I think it is also that you are offering something completely home-made that you have taken time and trouble over in an age where so many meals have to be put together in minutes, quite often from packets from the pantry or freezer.

SPECIAL OCCASIONS AND TRADITIONAL IDEAS

Not that all the tarts and pies in this book take an age to make, far from it. I hope that when you dip into these recipes you will find plenty of ideas for pastries that can be made quickly and easily with satisfying results. There are quick crumb crusts melted together in minutes, as well as a clutch of pies and tarts using ready made puff and filo pastries.

For special occasions you will find more fanciful creations copiously decorated with pastry leaves, stars and lattice work patterns or finished with wafer thin slices of fruit glazed with a shiny lacquer of glistening jam or fruit purée. Traditional favourites,

such as French Apple Flan (page 36), Game Pie (page 127), Steak and Kidney Pie (page 113) and, of course, Treacle Tart (page 16) have not been forgotten and there are tarts and pies for all seasons, too.

SPRING

In Spring, when home grown fruits and vegetables are sadly thin on the ground, there are plenty of dishes to be made with exotic fruits, dried fruits, chocolate and even the neglected banana. Try Chocolate Swirl Tart (page 42) for a rich and creamy treat, Mango Star Pie (page 76) or Banoffi Pie (page 13). When the first shallots of the season, appear, enjoy Onion Tart Tatin (page 46).

SUMMER

Summer is a time of plenty, with an amazing choice of soft fruits and vegetables at their cheapest and best. Celebrate the short asparagus season with Asparagus, Parmesan and Egg Tart (page 59) made large for a delicious lunch, or small as picnic fare. Make the most of the first strawberries with stunning Strawberry Crumble Flan (page 10), made in minutes with a ginger biscuit base and soft creamy filling, or round off a special summer dinner party with a

wonderful Raspberry Brûlée Tart (page 15).

AUTUMN

Autumn has particular pleasures. Who does not look forward to seeing the arrival of pumpkins, plums, apples from Kent orchards and new season mushrooms. Spend a day in the kitchen stocking up the freezer (or the family!) with the likes of Apple and Orange Sponge Tart (page 25), Potato Tart with Ham, Artichokes and Mushrooms (page 75), Toffee Apple Pie (page 82) and Pecan Pie (page 87) to name just a few. Autumn Fruit Cobbler (page 91) is one of my special favourites.

CHRISTMAS

Pies and tarts are welcome on any and every occasion, from lazy summer picnics to working lunches and fireside dinners, but at Christmas time when kitchen activity is often at its most feverish, they can really play a starring role.

Mince pies are a must, either made in the traditional way (page 89) or as a centrepiece studded with cranberries or clementines and finished off with pastry holly leaves (pages 23 and 89). Salmon in Puff Pastry (page 105) is perfect for a festive dinner and makes a welcome change from a diet dominated by meat and poultry. Celebrate the epiphany the French way with the delicious Gâteau Pithiviers (page 78). In France the baker buries a tiny figure in the filling of the gâteau. Whoever finds it in their portion is 'king' for the day.

VEGETARIANS

Vegetarians will find plenty of recipes to choose from within the pages of this book. While meat and fish are represented, there is plenty of scope for using seasonal produce, perhaps studded with nuts or seeds or strewn with fresh herbs, garlic, ginger or spices. I am sure you will enjoy trying, Grilled Pepper and Onion Tart (page 65), Three Tomato and Basil Tart (page 68) and Spiced Cauliflower Crumble Pie (page 111), to name just a few. Many of the dishes offer one or two variations, giving plenty of scope for experiment. A huge amount of work and thought has gone into the writing of this book and every recipe has been tested and tasted to make sure it works well for you. It has been a tremendously satisfying and rewarding task and I hope you will find the results an inspiration.

THE INGREDIENTS
FLOUR

For traditional crisp short pastry plain flour is the best choice. However, some cooks prefer the more scone-like result obtained by using self raising flour. Wholemeal flour gives a crumbly nutty-flavoured pastry, although I find it hard to work with and roll out when used on its own. For easy handling use equal proportions of wholemeal and plain flour. For a yeast pastry, strong plain bread flour is the best choice as it contains a high level of gluten which gives the dough extra elasticity.

FAT

In many old recipes the fat used is half butter or margarine and half lard. The butter gives the pastry its rich flavour and golden colour and the lard adds a short crumbly texture. I find lard too oily and heavy for my taste and prefer to use all butter, but the choice is yours. For rich flan pastries use all butter.

The normal ratio of fat to flour is half the weight of fat to flour, although for some of the richer doughs the fat is increased slightly. This sometimes makes the pastry a little softer than normal, so it should be chilled before rolling out to make handling easier.

The fat should always be cold for best results, but it should be removed from the refrigerator shortly before use to make it easier to handle.

WATER

Use as little water as possible to bind the dough. Adding too much water can make the dough sticky and difficult to handle and the cooked pastry tough. Always try to use cold water, or iced water in warm weather. For normal shortcrust pastry you will need about 1 teaspoon of water for each 25 g/1 oz of flour used. This varies a little depending on the absorbency of the flour, but it is a useful guideline to follow. If you are adding egg or egg yolk to the pastry use proportionately less water.

SUGAR

Some rich pastries use a small amount of sugar to give a crisp texture and golden colour. Stir in the sugar after rubbing in the flour, and before adding the liquid.

EGGS

Egg is used to bind rich pastries. Usually only the egg yolk is added.

PUFF PASTRY

Puff Pastry can be made at home but it takes a lot of skill, patience and understanding to achieve acceptable results. Ready made chilled or frozen puff pastry is usually of excellent quality and gives reliable quality every time.

FILO PASTRY

Filo Pastry can be bought chilled or frozen. It consists of paper-thin sheets layered on top of each other and rolled up. Thaw the pastry thoroughly before use, then unwrap carefully. On contact with air, the pastry can become very brittle and hard to manage, so any sheets not actually being used should be kept covered with a damp cloth or clingfilm. Any leftover sheets can be tightly wrapped in clingfilm and stored in the refrigerator for up to 2 days.

ROLLING OUT
Knead the pastry as quickly and lightly as possible on a lightly floured surface. Take care to use as little extra flour as possible. Too much flour can upset the proportions of the pastry, with tough results.

Roll out the pastry lightly and evenly, using short sharp strokes of the rolling pin. Turn the pastry as you work, bearing in mind the final shape you need, to avoid waste. Roll the pastry away from you, and turn it in one direction only.

BAKING
Pastries need a fairly hot oven to turn the water swiftly into steam. This makes the pastry light, and gives the pastry a good colour.

LINING A FLAN TIN

1 Set the flan tin or ring on a baking sheet. This will help to transfer the heat to the base of the flan.
2 Roll out the pastry to about 2.5 cm/1 inch larger than the flan tin. Support the pastry over the rolling pin and lift it onto the flan tin.
3 Ease the pastry into the tin, pressing it into the corners and flutes of the tin. This will help to prevent the pastry from shrinking too much.
4 Roll the rolling pin over the top of the tin to trim off the excess pastry. Press the pastry into the flutes again.
5 Prick the base of the pastry with a fork several times. Chill for 30 minutes before baking to set the pastry and reduce shrinkage.

BAKING BLIND
Flan cases are often either partly or completely baked before the filling is added to ensure crisp results.

1 Line the flan case with a large circle of greaseproof paper. Fill with baking beans, pulses or pasta (these can be saved and used again for the same purpose).
2 Bake in a preheated oven for 10-15 minutes or for the time indicated in individual recipes, then remove the paper and beans and return the flan case to the oven for 5 minutes. Note: If preferred, the greaseproof paper and beans can be replaced with a piece of crumpled foil.

COVERING A PIE

1 Roll out the pastry to measure 5 cm/2 inches larger all round than the pie dish. Cut off a 2.5 cm/1 inch strip all round.
2 Brush the rim of the pie dish with water and attach the pastry strip, trimming it to fit.
3 Brush the pastry strip with water, then cover the pie filling with the pastry, pressing the edges of lid and pastry strip together to seal.
4 Make a hole in the centre of the pastry lid to allow steam to escape.
5 If time permits, chill the pie for 30 minutes before baking.

MAKING DECORATIVE EDGES

FLUTED EDGE FOR A DOUBLE CRUST PIE
1 Using the blunt side of a knife, make several blunt cuts all round the cut edges of the pastry.

2 Pinch the pastry rim at 2.5 cm/ 1 inch intervals between the thumb and forefinger, while lifting the pastry edge with a knife.

PINCHED EDGE FOR TART OR PIE
Place the forefinger of your left hand on the inside edge of the pastry rim and pinch the pastry around it with the thumb and forefinger of your right hand. Continue around the edge of the tart or pie.

ZIG-ZAG EDGE FOR A TART
1 Make cuts around the pastry rim at 2.5 cm/1 inch intervals.
2 Brush the rim with water, then fold each cut piece in half diagonally to form triangular shapes.

MAKING A PASTRY LATTICE
1 Line the pie plate with pastry, reserve the pastry trimmings and fill the pie with the chosen filling. Roll out the pastry trimmings thinly and cut into 1 cm/½ inch wide strips.
2 Dampen the edges of the pastry case and lay a pastry strip across one side of the tart, pressing the edges to seal.
3 Lay a second strip of pastry at right angles to the first. Continue attaching pastry strips alternately at right angles, leaving even-sized gaps between each strip. The strips may be twisted, if preferred.
4 Trim off excess pastry.

MAKING PASTRY LEAVES
1 Roll out the pastry thinly and cut into a 2.5 cm/1 inch wide strip.
2 Cut diagonally across the strip at 2.5 cm/1 inch intervals to form diamond shapes.
3 Mark the veins of the leaves with the tip of a knife.
4 Brush the top of the pie with a little water and attach the leaves.
5 Glaze as you wish.

STORING PASTRY
Made up uncooked dough can be stored in the refrigerator for up to 2 days. Wrap it tightly in a polythene bag or foil and remove it from the refrigerator for 30 minutes before shaping. Alternatively, the uncooked pastry case can be stored for the same time, ready for baking.

FREEZING PASTRY
Pastry is best frozen ready shaped, whether cooked or uncooked. Freeze pastry cases or pies in foil containers, or freezerproof dishes. Empty pastry cases can be cooked from frozen, adding an extra 5 minutes to the conventional cooking time. Filled pies are best thawed before baking to ensure they are cooked through. Store for up to 3 months.

STORING RUBBED IN PASTRY MIXTURE
Rubbed in pastry mixture can be stored in the refrigerator for up to 1 week. Alternatively, it may be frozen for 3 months. Thaw before adding the water.

USING A FOOD PROCESSOR
You can get excellent results when making pastry in a food processor, especially if the weather is hot or you have warm hands. If you have one use the pulse button to ensure the mixture is not overworked, and measure the water carefully. You may need to add more water than if you were making pastry by hand.

Strawberry Crumble Flan

CRUMB CASE:
175 g/6 oz ginger biscuits
75 g/3 oz butter

FILLING:
250 g/8 oz cream cheese, softened
75 g/3 oz caster sugar
1 teaspoon grated lemon rind
4 tablespoons single cream
375 g/12 oz small strawberries, hulled, halved if large
icing sugar, for dusting

1 Crumb the ginger biscuits in a food processor. Alternatively, place the biscuits between 2 large sheets of greaseproof paper and crush them with a heavy rolling pin. Melt the butter in a small saucepan, add the biscuit crumbs and mix well.

2 Press the crumb mixture over the base and sides of a loose-bottomed 20 cm/8 inch flan tin. Chill until set.

3 Beat the cream cheese, caster sugar, grated lemon rind and cream in a bowl. Carefully transfer the chilled crumb crust from the flan tin to a serving plate. Fill the case with the cream cheese mixture, smoothing the top.

4 Arrange the strawberries on top of the cream cheese mixture. Dust with icing sugar and serve cold.

Serves 4-6
Preparation time: 20 minutes

Tart Tatin

This is my version of the classic French tart. It is deceptively simple to make and everyone loves it.

PASTRY:

175 g/6 oz plain flour
75 g/3 oz chilled butter, diced
25 g/1 oz caster sugar
1 egg yolk

FOR THE APPLES:

50 g/2 oz butter
50 g/2 oz caster sugar
6 eating apples, such as Cox's, peeled, cored and quartered

1 Place the flour in a bowl, add the diced butter and rub in with the fingertips until the mixture resembles fine breadcrumbs. Stir in the sugar. Add the egg yolk and enough water, about 2-3 tablespoons, to mix to a firm dough.

2 Prepare the apple mixture. Melt the butter and sugar in a 20 cm/8 inch ovenproof frying pan. When the mixture is golden, add the apples and toss them in the syrup to coat them. Cook for a few minutes, until the apples start to caramelize.

3 Roll out the pastry on a lightly floured surface to a round, a little larger than the pan. Place it over the apples, folding over the edges of the pastry until it fits the pan neatly.

4 Bake in a preheated oven, 200°C (400°F), Gas Mark 6 for 35-40 minutes, until the pastry is golden.

Cool in the pan for 5 minutes, place a large plate on top of the pan and invert the tart on to it. Serve warm with thick cream or crème fraîche.

Serves 4-6
Preparation time: 20 minutes
Cooking time: 35-40 minutes
Oven temperature: 200°C (400°F), Gas Mark 6

VARIATION

Pear and Walnut Tart

Replace the apples with 5 ripe pears and sprinkle with 50 g/2 oz of walnut halves before covering with the pastry. Then bake the tart as in the main recipe.

Banoffi Pie

CRUMB CASE:

250 g/8 oz digestive biscuits
125 g/4 oz butter

FILLING:

175 g/6 oz butter
175 g/6 oz caster sugar
1 x 425 g/14 oz can condensed milk
2 bananas
1 tablespoon lemon juice
150 ml/¼ pint whipping cream
25 g/1 oz dark chocolate, grated

1 Crumb the biscuits in a food processor or place between 2 sheets of greaseproof paper and crush with a rolling pin. Melt the butter in a pan and stir in the crumbs.
2 Press the mixture evenly over the base and sides of a deep 20 cm/8 inch round flan tin. Chill until firm.
3 Make the filling. Place the butter and sugar in a pan. Heat gently, stirring until the butter has melted. Stir in the condensed milk and bring to the boil. Lower the heat and simmer for 5 minutes, stirring occasionally, until the mixture becomes a caramel colour. Pour into the crumb base, cool, then chill until set.
4 Slice the bananas and toss them in the lemon juice. Reserve one-quarter of the bananas for decoration and spread the rest over the filling. Whip the cream and spread over the top. Decorate with the reserved bananas and sprinkle with chocolate.

Serves 6-8
Preparation time: 30 minutes, plus chilling time

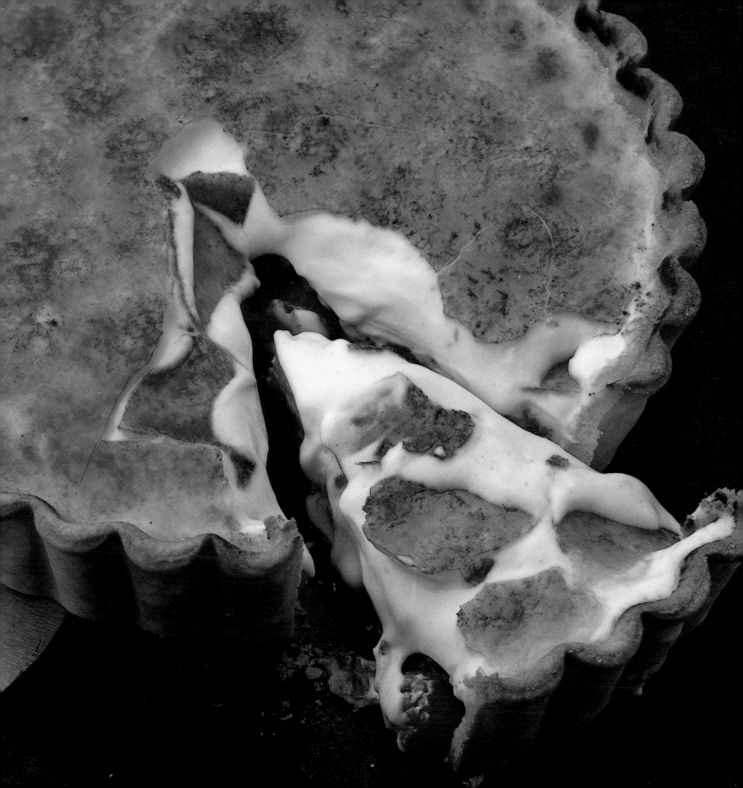

Raspberry Brûlée Tart

PASTRY:
175 g/6 oz plain flour
75 g/3 oz chilled butter, diced
25 g/1 oz caster sugar
1 egg, beaten

FILLING:
150 ml/¼ pint double cream
150 ml/¼ pint thick Greek yogurt
25 g/1 oz caster sugar
1 teaspoon grated orange rind
125 g/4 oz raspberries, hulled
50 g/2 oz golden granulated sugar

1 Measure the flour into a bowl, add the butter and rub in with the fingertips until the mixture resembles fine breadcrumbs. Stir in the sugar, then add the egg. Mix to a firm dough, adding a little water if necessary.

2 Turn the dough out on to a lightly floured surface and knead briefly. Roll out and line a 20 cm/8 inch deep flan tin. Chill for 30 minutes, if time permits, then fill with crumpled foil and bake in a preheated oven, 200°C (400°F), Gas Mark 6 for 15 minutes. Remove the foil and return the pastry case to the oven for 10 minutes, until the pastry is cooked and golden brown.

3 Make the filling. Whip the cream in a bowl until stiff, then carefully fold in the yogurt, caster sugar and orange rind. Arrange the raspberries over the base of the flan case and cover with the cream mixture. Chill for about 1 hour until firm.

4 Sprinkle the golden granulated sugar evenly over the filling, taking care to leave none of the cream mixture exposed. Protect the pastry edges with a strip of foil, then place the tart under a preheated hot grill until the sugar is melted and bubbling. Cool, then chill until ready to serve.

Serves 4-6
Preparation time: 25 minutes, plus chilling time
Cooking time: 25 minutes
Oven temperature: 200°C (400°F), Gas Mark 6

VARIATIONS

Grape and Orange Brûlée Tart

Replace the raspberries with 125 g/4 oz seedless grapes and 1 orange, peeled and segmented.

Dried Apricot Brûlée Tart

Replace the raspberries with 75 g/3 oz ready-to-eat dried apricots, chopped. Fold the apricots into the cream with ½ teaspoon ground cinnamon, proceed as main recipe.

Treacle Tart

This old nursery favourite is hard to beat on a cold winter's day. Serve it with custard or whipped cream after a leisurely Sunday lunch.

PASTRY:
250 g/8 oz plain flour
125 g/4 oz chilled butter, diced
FILLING:
175 g/6 oz golden syrup
125 g/4 oz fresh white breadcrumbs
grated rind and juice of 1 lemon

1 Place the flour in a bowl, add the butter and rub in with the fingertips until the mixture resembles breadcrumbs. Stir in enough cold water, about 3-4 tablespoons, to mix to a firm dough.
2 Turn out dough on a lightly floured surface and knead briefly. Roll out and line a 20 cm/8 inch deep flan tin. Trim the edges. Make cuts around the pastry rim at 2.5 cm/1 inch intervals. Brush rim with water then fold each piece in half to form triangular shapes (see page 9). Chill for 30 minutes if time permits.

3 Warm the syrup in a saucepan until it is runny, then remove the pan from the heat and stir in the breadcrumbs, lemon rind and juice. Spread over the pastry case.
4 Bake the tart in a preheated oven, 190°C (375°F), Gas Mark 5 for 30-35 minutes, until the pastry is crisp and the filling golden. Serve warm or cold.

Serves 6
Preparation time: 20 minutes
Cooking time: 30-35 minutes
Oven temperature: 190°C (375°F), Gas Mark 5

VARIATIONS

Fruity Treacle Tart

Add 75 g/3 oz mixed dried fruit to the golden syrup and bake as in the main recipe.

Apple Treacle Tart

Add 1 medium eating apple, peeled, cored and grated, to the golden syrup and bake as in the main recipe.

Dark Treacle Tart

Replace 1 tablespoon of the syrup with 1 tablespoon black treacle and bake as in the main recipe.

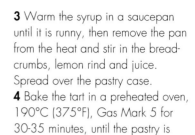

Pear, Red Wine and Walnut Tart

PASTRY:

175 g/6 oz plain flour
75 g/3 oz chilled butter, diced
50 g/2 oz caster sugar
25 g/1 oz walnuts, finely chopped
1 egg yolk

FOR THE PEARS:

4 ripe pears
1 tablespoon lemon juice
300 ml/½ pint red wine
125 g/4 oz caster sugar
1 cinnamon stick
4 tablespoons redcurrant jelly

FILLING:

150 ml/¼ pint thick cold custard
150 ml/¼ pint double cream

1 Measure the flour into a bowl, add the diced butter and rub in with the fingertips until the mixture resembles fine breadcrumbs. Stir in the caster sugar and chopped walnuts, then add the egg yolk. Mix to a firm dough, adding a little water if necessary.

2 Turn the dough out on to a lightly floured surface and knead briefly. Roll out and line a 23 cm/9 inch flan tin. Chill the pastry for 30 minutes, if time permits. Fill with crumpled foil and bake in a preheated oven, 200°C (400°F), Gas Mark 6 for 15 minutes. Remove the foil and bake the pastry case for 10 minutes more, until the pastry is crisp and golden brown.

3 Peel, halve and core the pears. Brush them with the lemon juice to prevent discolouring. Combine the wine, sugar and cinnamon stick in a large saucepan. Bring to the boil, add the pears and poach gently for about 10 minutes, until tender but still firm.

4 Using a slotted spoon, remove the pears and cinnamon stick from the syrup. Discard the cinnamon stick. Boil the syrup hard for about 10 minutes until thick and syrupy. Stir in the redcurrant jelly and continue to stir until smooth.

5 Brush the inside of the pastry case with a little of the red wine syrup. Whisk the custard in a large bowl for 2 minutes, until fluffy. Whip the cream in a separate bowl until stiff, then fold into the custard. Spread the mixture over the pastry case.

6 Slice the pears thinly, keeping their shape and arrange over the filling. Brush liberally with the remaining red wine syrup. Serve chilled.

Serves 6
Preparation time: 35 minutes
Cooking time: 25 minutes
Oven temperature: 200°C (400°F), Gas Mark 6

Brandied Prune Flan

PASTRY:

175 g/6 oz plain flour
75 g/3 oz chilled butter, diced
50 g/2 oz caster sugar
1 egg yolk

FILLING:

175 g/6 oz cream cheese
50 g/2 oz ground almonds
75 g/3 oz butter, softened
75 g/3 oz caster sugar
2 eggs, beaten
2 tablespoons brandy
175 g/6 oz stoned ready-to-eat prunes
2 tablespoons clear honey

1 Measure the flour into a bowl, add the butter and rub in with the fingertips until the mixture resembles fine breadcrumbs. Stir in the sugar, then add the egg yolk. Mix to a firm dough, adding a little water if necessary.

2 Turn the dough out on a lightly floured surface and knead briefly. Roll out and line a 23 cm/9 inch flan tin. Chill for 30 minutes, if time permits. Fill with crumpled foil and bake in a preheated oven 200°C (400°F), Gas Mark 6 for 15 minutes, then remove the foil and return to the oven for a further 5 minutes. Lower the oven temperature to 190°C (375°F), Gas Mark 5.

3 Make the filling. Beat the cream cheese, almonds, butter, sugar, eggs and brandy in a bowl. Spread the mixture over the pastry case and stud the top with the prunes. Bake for 25 minutes, until the filling is firm.

4 Warm the honey in a small saucepan and brush over the top of the flan. Serve warm or cold.

Serves 6-8
Preparation time: 30 minutes
Cooking time: 45 minutes
Oven temperature: 200°C (400°F), Gas Mark 6, then 190°C (375°F), Gas Mark 5

VARIATIONS

Damson Flan

Replace the prunes with 175 g/6 oz stoned fresh damsons and cook as for the main recipe.

Apricot Flan

Replace the prunes with 175 g/6 oz ready-to-eat dried apricots, chopped and folded into the filling mixture. Cook as for the main recipe.

Orange Tart

PASTRY:

175 g/6 oz plain flour
75 g/3 oz chilled butter, diced
50 g/2 oz caster sugar
1 egg yolk

FILLING:

2 eggs plus 2 egg yolks
150 g/5 oz caster sugar
150 ml/¼ pint single cream
3 oranges

TO DECORATE:

1 orange
75 g/3 oz caster sugar
3 tablespoons water
150 ml/¼ pint double cream

1 Put the flour into a bowl, add the butter and rub in with the fingertips until the mixture resembles fine bread-crumbs. Stir in the sugar, then add the egg yolk. Mix to a firm dough, adding a little water if necessary.
2 Turn the dough out on to a lightly floured surface and knead briefly. Roll out and line a 20 cm/8 inch deep flan tin. Chill for 30 minutes, if time permits, then fill with crumpled foil and bake in a preheated oven 200°C (400°F), Gas Mark 6 for 15 minutes. Remove foil and cook the pastry case for 5 minutes more. Reduce the oven temperature to 160°C (325°F), Gas Mark 3.
3 Make the filling. Whisk the eggs, egg yolks and sugar in a bowl until foamy. Whisk in the cream. Grate the rind from the 3 oranges and squeeze the juice from 1 of them.

Use the remaining oranges in another recipe; use soon as they deteriorate once the rind has been removed. Add the rind and juice to the egg mixture and whisk again. Pour into the pastry case and bake for 30-35 minutes, until filling is firm.
4 Prepare the decoration. Pare the rind from the orange: don't include any white pith. Cut the rind into thin strips. Place the sugar in a pan with the water. Bring to the boil, stirring until the sugar has dissolved. Add the orange rind and boil for 2-3 minutes without stirring, until syrupy.
5 Using a slotted spoon, transfer the orange rind from the syrup to a plate. Whip the double cream in a

bowl until stiff; use to decorate the rim of the tart. Sprinkle with the glazed orange rind and serve cold.

Serves 6
Preparation time: 30 minutes
Cooking time: 50-55 minutes
Oven temperature: 200°C (400°F), Gas Mark 6, then 160°C (325°F), Gas Mark 3

VARIATION

Lemon Tart

Replace the 3 oranges in the filling with the rind of 4 lemons and the juice of 2. Use a lemon instead of the orange for the decoration.

Summer Fruit Flan

This large summer flan filled with luscious berry fruits is perfect for entertaining as it looks very special and serves up to 10 people.

**500 g/1 lb puff pastry, thawed
   if frozen**
beaten egg, to glaze

CUSTARD FILLING:
1 egg
50 g/2 oz caster sugar
40 g/1½ oz plain flour
300 ml/½ pint milk
25 g/1 oz butter, diced
few drops of vanilla essence

TOPPING:
**250 g/8 oz strawberries, hulled
   and sliced**
125 g/4 oz raspberries, hulled
125 g/4 oz loganberries, hulled
250 g/8 oz cherries, stoned and halved
3 peaches, sliced
125 g/4 oz redcurrants, stemmed
125 g/4 oz blackcurrants, stemmed
**4 tablespoons redcurrant or
   bramble jelly**

1 Roll out the pastry on a lightly floured surface to a 30 cm/12 inch square. Place on a greased baking sheet. Trim off a 2.5 cm/1 inch strip from all sides, then brush the edges with egg. Place the strips on top of the pastry, around the edge, to form a case, trimming them to fit. Press down to seal, then pinch the edges to decorate.

2 Prick the base of the pastry all over with a fork, then brush the edges with egg. Bake in a preheated oven 220°C (425°F), Gas Mark 7 for 20 minutes, until pastry is risen and golden brown. Cool on a wire rack.

3 To make the filling, place the egg and sugar in a bowl and whisk until frothy. Whisk in the flour and 1 tablespoon of the milk. Heat the remaining milk in a saucepan; pour it into the mixture, stirring all the time.

4 Return the mixture to the pan and cook over a moderate heat, stirring until the custard is thick and smooth. Remove from the heat and beat in the butter and vanilla. Cover closely and leave to cool.

5 Spread the custard over the pastry case and group the fruit decoratively on the top. Warm the redcurrant or bramble jelly in a small pan and brush over the fruit and pastry edges. Chill for up to 2 hours before serving.

Serves 8-10
Preparation time: 30 minutes
Cooking time: 20 minutes
Oven temperature: 220°C (425°F),
Gas Mark 7

Festive Mincemeat Tart

PASTRY:

250 g/8 oz self-raising flour
125 g/4 oz chilled butter, diced
75 g/3 oz caster sugar
grated rind of 1 orange
1 egg, beaten
2-3 tablespoons milk

FILLING:

500 g/1 lb mincemeat

TO DECORATE:

milk, to glaze
caster sugar, for sprinkling

1 Measure the flour into a bowl, add the diced butter and rub in with the fingertips until the mixture resembles fine breadcrumbs. Stir in the caster sugar and grated orange rind, then add the beaten egg and enough milk to form a soft dough.

2 Turn the dough out on a lightly floured surface and knead briefly. Roll out and line a 25 x 15 cm/10 x 6 inch shallow rectangular tin. Trim the edges, reserving the trimmings.

3 Spread the mincemeat over the base of the pastry case. Reroll the reserved pastry trimmings and cut into small star shapes. Arrange the shapes over the mincemeat.

4 Brush the pastry with milk and sprinkle with a little sugar. Bake in a preheated oven, 190°C (375°F), Gas Mark 5 for 25-30 minutes, until the pastry is golden brown. Serve warm with cream or custard.

Serves 6-8
Preparation time: 20 minutes
Cooking time: 25-30 minutes
Oven temperature: 190°C (375°F), Gas Mark 5

VARIATIONS

Apple and Mincemeat Tart

Reduce the quantity of mincemeat to 375 g/12 oz and add 2 apples, peeled, cored and grated. Cook as for the main recipe.

Mincemeat and Cranberry Tart

Reduce the quantity of mincemeat to 250 g/8 oz and stir in 250 g/8 oz fresh or frozen cranberries. Cut the pastry trimmings into small Christmas tree or holly shapes to decorate. Cook as for the main recipe.

Latticed Jam Tart

It is worth making this simple tart with the best quality jam, preferably home-made.

250 g/8 oz plain flour
125 g/4 oz chilled butter, diced
250 g/8 oz jam (raspberry, strawberry, blackberry or plum)
beaten egg, to glaze

1 Measure the flour into a bowl, add the butter and rub in with the fingertips until the mixture resembles fine breadcrumbs. Stir in enough cold water, about 3-4 tablespoons, to mix to a firm dough.
2 Turn the dough out on to a lightly floured surface and knead briefly. Roll out and line a 23 cm/9 inch pie plate. Trim the edges, reserving the pastry trimmings.

3 Spread the jam over the base of the pastry. Roll out the trimmings and cut into thin strips. Dampen the edges of the pastry with water and arrange the strips over the top in a lattice design.
4 Brush the pastry with egg and bake in a preheated oven 200°C (400°F), Gas Mark 6 for 25-30 minutes, until the pastry is crisp and golden. Serve warm.

Serves 6
Preparation time: 15 minutes
Cooking time: 25-30 minutes
Oven temperature: 200°C (400°F), Gas Mark 6

VARIATION

Jam Tarts

Make the pastry as in the main recipe and stamp out 18 x 7.5 cm/ 3 inch rounds using a fluted cutter. Line bun tins with the pastry and place 1 teaspoon of jam in each. Bake at 200°C (400°F), Gas Mark 6 for 12-15 minutes, until the pastry is crisp and golden.

Apple and Orange Sponge Tart

PASTRY:

175 g/6 oz plain flour
75 g/3 oz chilled butter, diced
1 egg yolk

FILLING:

125 g/4 oz butter, softened
125 g/4 oz caster sugar
2 eggs
125 g/4 oz self-raising flour
grated rind and juice of 1 orange
3 small eating apples
2 tablespoons apricot jam

1 Place the flour in a bowl, add the butter and rub in with the fingertips until the mixture resembles fine breadcrumbs. Stir in the egg yolk and enough cold water, about 2-3 tablespoons, to mix to a firm dough.
2 Turn the dough out on to a lightly floured surface and knead briefly. Roll out and line a 23 cm/9 inch deep flan tin. Chill for 30 minutes.
3 Make the filling. Combine the butter, sugar, eggs, flour, orange rind and juice in a bowl. Beat together for 2-3 minutes until light and fluffy. Spread the mixture over the pastry case.
4 Peel, quarter and core the apples. Slice each quarter thinly and fan out slightly. Place one in the centre of the filling and space the rest out evenly around the edge.
5 Bake the tart in a preheated oven,

190°C (375°F), Gas Mark 5 for 35-40 minutes, until the pastry is golden and the filling set. Warm the jam in a saucepan, sieve it into a bowl, then brush it over the top of the tart. Serve warm or cold.

Serves 6-8
Preparation time: 20 minutes
Cooking time: 35-40 minutes
Oven temperature: 190°C (375°F), Gas Mark 5

Blueberry Shortcake Tart

PASTRY:

375 g/12 oz self-raising flour
175 g/6 oz chilled butter, diced
125 g/4 oz caster sugar
1 egg, beaten

FILLING:

250 g/8 oz fresh or frozen blueberries
25 g/1 oz sugar
milk, see method
50 g/2 oz flaked almonds

1 Place the flour in a bowl, add the butter and rub it in until the mixture resembles fine breadcrumbs. Stir in the caster sugar. Add the egg and mix to a firm dough, adding a little cold water, if necessary.

2 Roll out two-thirds of the pastry and use to line a greased 23 cm/9 inch tart tin. Spread the blueberries evenly over the pastry case and sprinkle with the sugar.

3 Roll out the remaining pastry and cut into thin strips. Brush the rim of the tart with water and arrange the pastry strips in a lattice pattern over the top. Brush the pastry with a little milk and sprinkle with the flaked almonds.

4 Bake in a preheated oven, 190°C (375°F), Gas Mark 5 for 30-35 minutes, until the pastry is golden and the blueberries are tender. Serve the tart warm or cold with cream or crème fraîche.

Serves 6
Preparation time: 25 minutes
Cooking time: 30-35 minutes
Oven temperature: 190°C (375°F), Gas Mark 5

VARIATIONS

Apricot Shortcake Tart

Replace the blueberries with 500 g/1 lb fresh apricots, halved and stoned. Sprinkle the fruit with 50-75 g/2-3 oz sugar. Cook as for the main recipe.

Raspberry and Lemon Shortcake Tart

Add the grated rind of 1 lemon to the pastry mix. Replace the blueberries with 375 g/12 oz fresh or frozen raspberries. Cook as for the main recipe.

Apricot and Lemon Tart

PASTRY:
175 g/6 oz plain flour
75 g/3 oz chilled butter, diced
50 g/2 oz caster sugar
1 egg, beaten

FILLING:
50 g/2 oz butter, at room temperature
50 g/2 oz caster sugar
50 g/2 oz semolina
grated rind of 1 lemon
1 egg, beaten
750 g/1½ lb ripe apricots, halved
    and stoned
4 tablespoons apricot jam

1 Place the flour in a bowl, add the diced butter and rub in with the fingertips until the mixture resembles fine breadcrumbs. Stir in the caster sugar and beaten egg and mix to a firm dough, adding a little water if necessary.

2 Knead the dough briefly on a lightly floured surface, then wrap closely and chill for 30 minutes. Roll out the pastry and use to line a 23 cm/9 inch flan tin. Prick the pastry base all over with a fork.

3 Make the filling. Beat the butter and the caster sugar together in a bowl until light and fluffy. Beat in the semolina, lemon rind and beaten egg, and then spread the mixture over the pastry base. Arrange the apricot halves over the top, cut sides down.

4 Bake the tart in a preheated oven, 190°C (375°F), Gas Mark 5 for 40-45 minutes, until the pastry is browned and the filling golden and set. Warm the jam in a small saucepan, then press it through a sieve into a bowl. Brush the apricot glaze over the top of the tart. Serve warm or cold, with lightly whipped cream if liked.

Serves 6-8
Preparation time: 30 minutes, plus chilling time
Cooking time: 40-45 minutes
Oven temperature: 190°C (375°F), Gas Mark 5

Bakewell Tart

Although probably not the authentic version of Bakewell tart, I hope you will like it as much as I do.

PASTRY:

175 g/6 oz plain flour
75 g/3 oz chilled butter, diced
1 egg yolk

FILLING:

3 tablespoons seedless raspberry jam
75 g/3 oz caster sugar
3 eggs
75 g/3 oz butter, melted
75 g/3 oz ground almonds
few drops of almond essence
25 g/1 oz flaked almonds
50 g/2 oz icing sugar, sifted
25 g/1 oz glacé cherries, chopped

1 Place the flour in a bowl, add the diced butter and rub in with the fingertips until the mixture resembles fine breadcrumbs. Stir in the egg yolk and enough cold water, about 2-3 tablespoons, to mix to a firm dough.

2 Turn the dough out on a lightly floured surface and knead briefly. Roll out and line a 23 cm/9 inch tart tin. Chill the pastry case for 30 minutes, if time permits.

3 Spread the jam over the base of the pastry. In a bowl, whisk the caster sugar with the eggs until light and fluffy. Whisk in the melted butter, then stir in the ground almonds and almond essence.

4 Pour the filling into the pastry case and sprinkle with the flaked almonds. Bake in a preheated oven, 190°C (375°F), Gas Mark 5 for 35-40 minutes, until the pastry is crisp and the filling set. Leave to cool.

5 In a small bowl, blend the icing sugar to a paste with a few drops of water. Drizzle the icing over the tart and scatter the cherries over the top.

Serves 6-8
Preparation time: 25 minutes
Cooking time: 35-40 minutes
Oven temperature: 190°C (375°F), Gas Mark 5

Mango Puff Tartlets

250 g/8 oz puff pastry, thawed
    if frozen
1 ripe mango
25 g/1 oz unsalted butter
4 teaspoons caster sugar
2 tablespoons apricot jam

1 Divide the puff pastry into quarters; roll out each piece to a 10 cm/4 inch round. Space the rounds on a greased baking sheet.
2 Peel the mango and cut it in half around the stone. Cut each half in half again. Slice the mango quarters thinly and arrange over the pastry rounds.
3 Dot some butter over each mango topping and sprinkle with the caster sugar. Bake in a preheated oven, 220°C (425°F), Gas Mark 7 for 12-15 minutes, until the pastry is risen and golden and the mango is tender.
4 Warm the apricot jam in a small saucepan, press it through a sieve into a bowl, then carefully brush over the top of each mango tartlet. Serve the tartlets warm.

Makes 4
Preparation time: 10 minutes
Cooking time: 12-15 minutes
Oven temperature: 220°C (425°F), Gas Mark 7

VARIATIONS

Peach Puff Tartlets

Replace the mango with 4 peach halves, skinned, sliced thinly and arranged as in the main recipe.

Pear Puff Tartlets

Replace the mango with 2 ripe pears, peeled, cored and halved, then sliced and arranged as in the main recipe.

Apple Puff Tartlets

Replace the mango with 2 eating apples, peeled, cored and halved, then sliced thinly and arranged as in the main recipe. Sprinkle with 1 tablespoon flaked almonds before baking.

Wholemeal Apple and Spice Tart

PASTRY:

375 g/12 oz self-raising wholemeal flour
2 teaspoons ground mixed spice
175 g/6 oz chilled butter, diced
125 g/4 oz light muscovado sugar
1 egg, beaten

FILLING:

3 eating apples
2 tablespoons lemon juice
25 g/1 oz light muscovado sugar
milk, see method
2 tablespoons apricot jam, warmed

1 Place the flour and mixed spice in a bowl, add the butter and rub it in until the mixture resembles breadcrumbs. Stir in the sugar. Add the egg and mix to a firm dough, adding a little cold water, if necessary.

2 Roll out two-thirds of the pastry and use to line a greased 23 cm/9 inch tart tin. Peel and core the apples. Slice them thinly into a bowl, then toss them in the lemon juice and sugar. Spread the apples over the pastry case.

3 Roll out the remaining pastry and cut into thin strips. Brush the rim of the tart with water and arrange the pastry strips in a lattice over the top.

4 Brush the pastry with a little milk and bake in a preheated oven, 190°C (375°F), Gas Mark 5 for 25-30 minutes, then remove the tart from the oven, brush with the jam and return to the oven for 5 minutes.

Serves 6
Preparation time: 25 minutes
Cooking time: 30-35 minutes
Oven temperature: 190°C (375°F), Gas Mark 5

Chocolate Crumb Tart with Exotic Fruit

CRUMB CASE:

175 g/6 oz chocolate digestive biscuits
75 g/3 oz butter
1 tablespoon golden syrup

FILLING:

300 ml/½ pint crème fraîche
selection of exotic fruit, such as
** pawpaw, pineapple, pomegranate,**
** star fruit, kumquat**
2 tablespoons redcurrant jelly
1 tablespoon lime juice

1 Crumb the biscuits in a food processor. Alternatively, place them between 2 sheets of greaseproof paper and crush with a rolling pin. Melt the butter with the syrup in a saucepan. Stir in the crumbs. Press the mixture on to the base and sides of a greased deep 20 cm/8 inch flan tin and chill until firm.
2 Remove the crumb case from the flan tin and place on a serving plate.
3 Fill the crumb case with crème fraîche then slice the fruit and arrange over the top. Warm the redcurrant jelly with the lime juice in a small saucepan and drizzle over the fruit. Chill the tart for up to 2 hours until ready to serve.

Serves 6
Preparation time: 20 minutes, plus chilling time

Chocolate Mousse Tartlets

Do make sure you buy the best quality cooking chocolate for these tartlets, as the flavour is crucial.

PASTRY:
250 g/8 oz plain flour
125 g/4 oz chilled butter, diced
50 g/2 oz caster sugar
1 egg, beaten

FILLING:
175 g/6 oz dark chocolate, broken
   into squares
2-3 tablespoons water
15 g/½ oz unsalted butter, diced
1 tablespoon brandy or Cointreau
3 eggs, separated
icing sugar, for dusting

1 Place the flour in a bowl, add the butter and rub in with the fingertips until the mixture resembles fine breadcrumbs. Stir in the sugar, then add the egg and mix to a firm dough, adding a little water if necessary.

2 Turn the dough out on a lightly floured surface and knead briefly. Roll out and line 8 x 7.5 cm/3 inch deep tartlet tins. Reroll the trimmings and line 2-3 more tins. Fill each with crumpled foil and place on a baking sheet. Bake in a preheated oven, 200°C (400°F), Gas Mark 6 for 15 minutes, then remove the foil and return the tartlets to the oven for 5 minutes. Leave to cool.

3 Make the filling. Place the chocolate in a heatproof bowl. Add the water. Set the bowl over a pan of hot water and leave until the chocolate has melted, stirring occasionally.

4 Remove the bowl from over the water and stir in the butter until it has melted. Add the brandy or Cointreau. Stir in the egg yolks. Whisk the egg whites in a grease-free bowl until they are stiff and dry; fold into the chocolate mixture.

5 Spoon the mousse mixture into the pastry cases, then transfer to the refrigerator for 2-3 hours, until set. Dust the tartlets lightly with sifted icing sugar before serving. Serve cold.

Makes 10-11
Preparation time: 25 minutes, plus chilling time
Cooking time: 20 minutes
Oven temperature: 200°C (400°F), Gas Mark 6

French Apple Flan

Each region of France seems to have its own way of cooking the very popular apple flan.

PASTRY:
250 g/8 oz plain flour
150 g/5 oz chilled butter, diced
50 g/2 oz caster sugar
1 egg, beaten

FILLING:
750 g/1½ lb eating apples
3 tablespoons lemon juice
4 tablespoons warmed, sieved
    apricot jam
175 ml/6 fl oz single cream
2 eggs, beaten
50 g/2 oz caster sugar

1 Place the flour in a bowl, add the butter and rub in with the fingertips until the mixture resembles fine breadcrumbs. Stir in the sugar, then add the egg yolk and enough cold water, about 2-3 tablespoons, to mix to a firm dough.

2 Turn the dough out on a lightly floured surface and knead briefly. Roll out and line a 25 cm/10 inch flan tin. Chill the pastry case for 30 minutes, if time permits.

3 Make the filling. Peel and core the apples. Slice them thinly into a bowl and toss with the lemon juice. Drain the apples and arrange them in concentric circles over the base of the pastry case. Brush with the apricot jam. Bake in a preheated oven, 220°C (425°F), Gas Mark 7 for 10 minutes. Lower the oven temperature to 190°C (375°F), Gas Mark 5.

4 Whisk the cream, eggs and sugar in a bowl. Pour the mixture carefully over the apples. Return the flan to the oven for 30-35 minutes, until the pastry is golden and the filling cooked. Serve warm.

Serves 8
Preparation time: 30 minutes
Cooking time: 40-45 minutes
Oven temperature: 220°C (425°F), Gas Mark 7, then 190°C (375°F), Gas Mark 5

Hazelnut and Summer Fruit Tartlets

125 g/4 oz butter, softened
125 g/4 oz caster sugar
125 g/4 oz ground hazelnuts
250 g/8 oz mascarpone cheese
175 g/6 oz strawberries, raspberries or redcurrants

1 Beat the softened butter and caster sugar in a bowl for about 5 minutes until light and fluffy. Beat in the ground hazelnuts.

2 Grease 2 x 12-hole bun tins. Place a heaped teaspoon of mixture into each. Bake in a preheated oven, 180°C (350°F), Gas Mark 4 for 5-7 minutes or until the mixture has risen up the sides of the tins.

3 Cool the tartlet cases in the tins for 2 minutes, then remove carefully and cool on a wire rack. Just before serving, fill each tartlet with mascarpone cheese and top with a few pieces of fruit.

Makes 18-20
Preparation time: 20 minutes
Cooking time: 5-7 minutes
Oven temperature: 180°C (350°F), Gas Mark 4

Banana, Pineapple and Coconut Flapjack Tart

PASTRY:

175 g/6 oz plain flour

1 teaspoon ground cinnamon

75 g/3 oz chilled butter, diced

25 g/1 oz desiccated coconut

1 egg yolk

FILLING:

1 x 425 g/14 oz can pineapple chunks, drained

2 bananas, sliced thickly

25 g/1 oz caster sugar

2 tablespoons orange juice

50 g/2 oz butter

2 tablespoons golden syrup

50 g/2 oz light muscovado sugar

50 g/2 oz porridge oats

25 g/1 oz desiccated coconut

1 teaspoon ground cinnamon

1 Place the flour and cinnamon in a bowl, add the butter and rub in with the fingertips until the mixture resembles fine breadcrumbs. Add the desiccated coconut. Stir in the egg yolk and enough cold water, about 2-3 tablespoons, to mix to a firm dough.

2 Knead the dough briefly on a lightly floured surface, then roll out and line a 20 cm/8 inch pie plate. If liked, make a zig zag edge (see page 9). Fill with crumpled foil and bake in a preheated oven, 200°C (400°F), Gas Mark 6 for 15 minutes. Lower the oven temperature to 180°C (350°F), Gas Mark 4.

3 Fill the pie case with the pineapple chunks and banana slices and sprinkle with the caster sugar and orange juice.

4 Heat the butter, syrup and muscovado sugar in a saucepan, stirring until the butter and syrup have melted to form a smooth sauce. Remove the pan from the heat and stir in the oats, desiccated coconut and ground cinnamon.

5 Spread the oat mixture over the fruit, return the tart to the oven and bake for 20-25 minutes, until the flapjack topping has browned and the fruit is tender. Cover the surface with a sheet of foil if the flapjack becomes too brown. Serve warm or cold.

Serves 4-6

Preparation time: 25 minutes

Cooking time: 35-40 minutes

Oven temperature: 200°C (400°F), Gas Mark 6, then 180°C (350°F), Gas Mark 4

VARIATIONS

Plum Flapjack Tart

Replace the pineapple chunks and bananas with 500 g/1 lb plums, halved and stoned. Replace 25 g/1 oz of the desiccated coconut with 25 g/1 oz of the oats and proceed as main recipe.

Gooseberry and Ginger Tart

Replace the plums with 500 g/1 lb gooseberries, and add 1 teaspoon ground ginger to the flapjack mixture when stirring in the oats. Proceed as main recipe.

Peach and Almond Tart

PASTRY:

175 g/6 oz plain flour
75 g/3 oz chilled butter, diced
2 egg yolks

FILLING:

2 tablespoons bramble jelly
2 egg whites
75 g/3 oz caster sugar
50 g/2 oz ground almonds
25 g/1 oz chopped toasted almonds
few drops almond essence
4 small peaches, halved, stoned and
   sliced thickly

1 Place the flour in a bowl, add the butter and rub in with the fingertips until the mixture resembles fine breadcrumbs. Stir in the egg yolks and a little cold water if necessary and mix to a firm dough.

2 Turn the dough out on a lightly floured surface and knead briefly. Roll out and line a 23 cm/9 inch deep flan tin. Chill for 30 minutes, if time permits.

3 Fill the pastry case with crumpled foil and bake in a preheated oven 200°C (400°F), Gas Mark 6 for 15 minutes, then remove the foil and bake the pastry case for a further 5 minutes. Lower the oven temperature to 180°C (350°F), Gas Mark 4.

4 Spread the bramble jelly over the base of the pastry case. In a grease-free bowl, whisk the egg whites until stiff and dry. Whisk in 1 tablespoon of the sugar, then fold in the remainder with the ground almonds, toasted almonds and almond essence. Spread the filling over the tart case.

5 Arrange the peaches in a haphazard fashion over the filling. Bake for 30-35 minutes, until the filling is set and golden brown. Serve warm or cold.

Serves 6
Preparation time: 25 minutes
Cooking time: 50-55 minutes
Oven temperature: 200°C (400°F), Gas Mark 6, then 180°C (350°F), Gas Mark 4

Lemon Curd Tarts

PASTRY:

175 g/6 oz plain flour
75 g/3 oz chilled butter, diced

FILLING:

4 tablespoons lemon curd
250 g/8 oz curd cheese, softened
2 eggs, beaten
50 g/2 oz caster sugar
grated nutmeg, for sprinkling
icing sugar, for dusting

1 Place the flour in a bowl, add the butter and rub in with the fingertips until the mixture resembles fine breadcrumbs. Stir in enough cold water, about 2-3 tablespoons, to mix to a firm dough.

2 Turn out the dough on a lightly floured surface and knead briefly. Roll out and use to line 12 tartlet tins. Place a teaspoon of lemon curd in the base of each pastry case.

3 Beat the curd cheese, eggs and sugar in a bowl. Divide the filling between the pastry cases and sprinkle with grated nutmeg. Bake in a preheated oven, 190°C (375°F), Gas Mark 5 for 20-25 minutes, until the filling has risen and the pastry is crisp.

4 Dust with sifted icing sugar and serve warm or cold.

Makes 12
Preparation time: 20 minutes
Cooking time: 20-25 minutes
Oven temperature: 190°C (375°F), Gas Mark 5

Chocolate Swirl Tart

CRUMB CASE:
125 g/4 oz digestive biscuits
50 g/2 oz amaretti biscuits
75 g/3 oz butter

FILLING:
200 g/7 oz dark chocolate
300 ml/½ pint double cream

1 Crumb the biscuits in a food processor. Alternatively, place them between 2 sheets of greaseproof paper and crush with a rolling pin. Melt the butter in a saucepan and stir in the crumbs. Press the mixture into a greased 23 cm/ 9 inch pie plate. Leave to chill in the refrigerator until firm.
2 Break up the chocolate and place in a heatproof bowl over a pan of hot, not boiling, water. Stir gently until the chocolate has melted. Cover a rolling pin with foil and brush lightly with oil. Drizzle a little chocolate from the tip of a teaspoon or a small piping bag on to the rolling pin in zig-zag lines about 2.5 cm/1 inch long. Chill until set.
3 Whip the cream until stiff and fold into the remaining melted chocolate. Do not over fold as you want a swirled effect. Spoon into the chilled crumb case and chill for about 2 hours, until set.
4 Just before serving, carefully peel the chocolate decorations from the foil and pile into the centre of the tart.

Serves 6-8
Preparation time: 20 minutes, plus chilling time

Crystallized Fruit Flan

CRUMB CASE:
175 g/6 oz digestive biscuits
75 g/3 oz butter

FILLING:
250 g/8 oz cream cheese, softened
75 g/3 oz caster sugar
1 teaspoon grated lemon rind
4 tablespoons single cream
175 g/6 oz thinly sliced mixed crystallized fruit
icing sugar, for dusting

1 Crumb the biscuits in a food processor. Alternatively, place them between 2 large sheets of grease-proof paper and crush them with a rolling pin. Melt the butter in a saucepan, add the biscuit crumbs and mix well.
2 Press the crumb mixture over the base and sides of a loose-bottomed 20 cm/8 inch flan tin. Chill until the base is set.
3 Beat the cream cheese, caster sugar, lemon rind and cream in a bowl. Carefully transfer the crumb case from the flan tin to a serving plate. Fill the crumb case with the cream cheese mixture, smoothing the top.
4 Arrange the crystallized fruit attractively on top of the cream cheese mixture and serve the flan cold.

Serves 4-6
Preparation time: 20 minutes

Pear and Almond Tart

PASTRY:
175 g/6 oz plain flour
75 g/3 oz chilled butter, diced
FILLING:
50 g/2 oz butter
50 g/2 oz caster sugar
50 g/2 oz ground almonds
few drops almond essence
1 egg, beaten
2 ripe pears, quartered and sliced
2 tablespoons clear honey

1 Place the flour in a bowl, add the butter and rub in with the fingertips until the mixture resembles fine breadcrumbs. Stir in 3-4 tablespoons cold water and mix to a firm dough.
2 Turn the dough out on to a lightly floured surface and knead briefly. Roll out and line a 20 cm/8 inch flan tin.
3 Beat together the butter and sugar for about 5 minutes, until light and fluffy. Beat in the almonds, almond essence and egg and mix well. Spread over the pastry case.
4 Arrange the pears over the filling in a haphazard way, pressing them gently into the filling. Bake in a preheated oven, 180°C (350°F) Gas Mark 4 for 35-40 minutes, until the pastry is cooked and golden brown.
5 Warm the honey and brush over the tart. Serve warm or cold.

Serves 4
Preparation time: 25 minutes
Cooking time: 35-40 minutes
Oven temperature: 180°C (350°F), Gas Mark 4

SAVOURY TARTS

Onion Tart Tatin

PASTRY:
175 g/6 oz self-raising wholemeal flour
75 g/3 oz chilled butter, diced
2 tablespoons chopped fresh parsley
2 teaspoons chopped fresh thyme
2-3 tablespoons lemon juice

TOPPING:
500 g/1 lb shallots, peeled
25 g/1 oz butter
2 tablespoons olive oil
2 teaspoons muscovado sugar
salt and pepper

1 Place the flour in a bowl. Add the butter and rub in until the mixture resembles breadcrumbs. Stir in the remaining pastry ingredients and mix to a firm dough. Knead briefly.

2 Make the topping. Boil the shallots in a pan of water for 10 minutes, then drain well. Heat the butter and oil in an ovenproof frying pan, add the shallots and fry gently, stirring, for about 10 minutes, until they are starting to colour. Sprinkle over the sugar, season to taste, and cook gently for a further 5 minutes, until the shallots are well coloured. Remove the pan from the heat.

3 Roll out the dough on a floured surface to a round, a little larger than the pan. Support the dough over the rolling pin and place it over the shallots, tucking the edges of the pastry down the side of the pan. Bake the tart in a preheated oven, 200°C (400°F), Gas Mark 6 for 20-25 minutes, until the pastry is crisp.

4 Cool the tart in the pan for 5 minutes, then place a large plate over the pan and invert the tart on to it. Serve warm or cold.

Serves 4-6
Preparation time: 30 minutes
Cooking time: 20-25 minutes
Oven temperature: 200°C (400°F), Gas Mark 6

Garden Vegetable Tart

PASTRY:

175 g/6 oz plain flour
25 g/1 oz ground hazelnuts
125 g/4 oz chilled butter, diced
2 tablespoons grated Parmesan cheese

FILLING:

125 g/4 oz soft cheese with garlic and herbs
150 ml/¼ pint milk
2 eggs, beaten
500 g/1 lb cooked chopped vegetables (baby carrots, mange tout, leeks, asparagus)
125 g/4 oz cherry tomatoes
salt and pepper

1 Mix the flour and hazelnuts in a bowl. Add the butter and rub in with the fingertips until the mixture resembles fine breadcrumbs. Stir in the Parmesan, then add enough cold water, about 2-3 tablespoons, to mix to a firm dough.

2 Turn the dough out on a lightly floured surface and knead briefly. Roll out and line a 23 cm/9 inch pie plate. Fill with crumpled foil and bake in a preheated oven, 200°C (400°F), Gas Mark 6 for 15 minutes. Remove the foil and bake the pastry case for 5 minutes more. Lower the oven temperature to 180°C (350°F), Gas Mark 4.

3 Make the filling. Combine the cheese, milk and eggs in a blender or food processor; process until smooth. Season with salt and pepper. Fill the pastry case with the vegetables, then pour over the filling. Bake the tart for 25 minutes, until the filling is firm. Serve warm or cold.

Serves 6

Preparation time: 25 minutes
Cooking time: 45 minutes
Oven temperature: 200°C (400°F), Gas Mark 6, then 180°C (350°F), Gas Mark 4

Salami and Olive Tart

YEAST PASTRY:

250 g/8 oz strong white flour
1 teaspoon easy-blend yeast
1 teaspoon salt
150 ml/¼ pint hand-hot water
1 tablespoon olive oil

TOPPING:

1 x 250 g/8 oz can chopped tomatoes
1 tablespoon tomato purée
2 teaspoons dried oregano
125 g/4 oz sliced salami
75 g/3 oz black olives, stoned
salt and pepper

1 Mix the flour, yeast and salt in a bowl. Add the water and oil and mix quickly to a soft dough. Turn out on to a lightly floured surface and knead for 5 minutes. Place the dough in a large oiled polythene bag, tie the top loosely and leave to rise for 30 minutes.

2 Make the topping. Combine the chopped tomatoes and tomato purée in a small saucepan. Add 1 teaspoon of the oregano, with salt and pepper to taste. Bring to the boil, stirring, then lower the heat and simmer the tomato mixture for about 5 minutes, until thickened. Leave to cool.

3 Roll out the pastry on a lightly floured surface and line a 33 x 23 cm/13 x 9 inch greased Swiss roll tin. Spread with the tomato topping and arrange the salami

slices on top. Sprinkle over the olives and remaining oregano.

4 Bake the tart in a preheated oven, 220°C (425°F), Gas Mark 7 for 20-25 minutes, until the pastry edges are crisp and golden brown. Serve the tart warm.

Serves 4-6

Preparation time: 45 minutes
Cooking time: 20-25 minutes
Oven temperature: 220°C (425°F), Gas Mark 7

Goats' Cheese and Cherry Tomato Puff Tart

Serve this delicious tart hot either as a starter or for a light lunch accompanied by a salad of bitter leaves.

250 g/8 oz puff pastry, thawed
    if frozen
olive oil, see method
250 g/8 oz cherry tomatoes,
    preferably a mixture of red and
    yellow, sliced

250 g/8 oz firm goats' cheese, sliced
2 teaspoons chopped fresh thyme
salt and pepper

1 Roll out the pastry on a lightly floured surface and trim to a 23 cm/9 inch round. Place on a greased baking sheet and brush lightly with olive oil.
2 Spread half the cherry tomatoes over the pastry to within 2.5 cm/1 inch of the edge. Arrange the goats' cheese over the top and sprinkle with the remaining tomatoes. Season with a little salt and pepper. Sprinkle with the thyme and drizzle 1-2 tablespoons of olive oil over the top.
3 Bake in a preheated oven, 220°C (425°F), Gas Mark 7 for 20-25 minutes, until the pastry is risen, crisp and golden brown.

Serves 4-6
Preparation time: 15 minutes
Cooking time: 20-25 minutes
Oven temperature: 220°C (425°F), Gas Mark 7

VARIATIONS

Goats' Cheese and Tomato Puff Tartlets

To make individual tartlets, cut the pastry into 7.5 cm/3 inch rounds and top as in the main recipe. Bake for 10-15 minutes.

Mozzarella and Pesto Puff Tart

250 g/8 oz puff pastry, thawed
    if frozen
olive oil, see method
3 tablespoons ready-made pesto
175 g/6 oz mozzarella cheese, sliced
2 shallots, sliced
1 tablespoon pine nuts

1 Roll out the pastry on a lightly floured surface and trim to a 23 cm/9 inch round. Place on a greased baking sheet and brush lightly with olive oil. Spread with the pesto to within 2.5 cm/1 inch of the edge. Arrange the mozzarella over the top.
2 Heat 1 tablespoon of olive oil in a small frying pan and fry the shallots for about 5 minutes until softened and lightly browned. Sprinkle over the tart, with the pine nuts. Bake as in main recipe.
(See photograph left.)

Courgette and Red Pepper Tart

PASTRY:
175 g/6 oz plain flour
1 teaspoon paprika
75 g/3 oz chilled butter, diced
FILLING:
2 tablespoons olive oil
2 red peppers, cored, seeded and
    chopped
375 g/12 oz courgettes, trimmed
2 eggs, beaten
300 ml/½ pint milk
50 g/2 oz mature Cheddar cheese,
    grated
salt and pepper

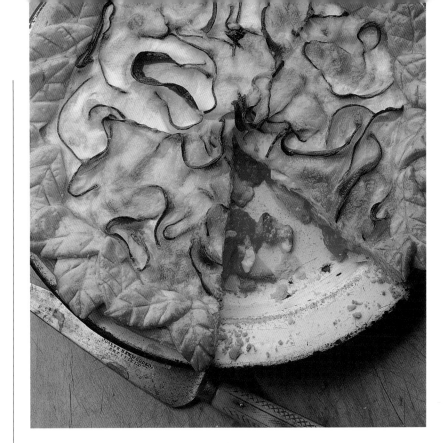

1 Measure the flour into a bowl and stir in the paprika. Add the butter and rub in with the fingertips until the mixture resembles fine breadcrumbs. Add enough cold water, about 2-3 tablespoons, to mix to a firm dough.
2 Turn out the dough on to a lightly floured surface and knead briefly. Roll out and line a 23 cm/9 inch pie plate. Roll out the pastry trimmings, cut them into leaf shapes and stick around the rim of the tart with a little water. Chill the pastry case for 30 minutes if time permits. Fill with crumpled foil and bake in a preheated oven 200°C (400°F), Gas Mark 6 for 15 minutes. Set the pastry case aside. Lower the oven temperature to 180°C (350°F), Gas Mark 4.
3 Make the filling. Heat the oil in a small frying pan, add the peppers and then cook gently for about 10 minutes, until softened. Season with salt and pepper, then purée in a blender or food processor. Alternatively, press the peppers through a sieve into a bowl.
4 Using a potato peeler, cut the courgettes into ribbons. Cook them in a saucepan of salted boiling water for 2 minutes, then drain and refresh under cold water. Drain the courgette ribbons again and pat dry with paper towels.
5 Beat the eggs, milk and cheese in a bowl. Add salt and pepper to taste. Spread the pepper purée over the base of the tart. Arrange the courgette ribbons evenly over the top and pour over the milk mixture. Bake for 25 minutes, until the filling is set and golden brown. Serve the tart warm or cold.

Serves 6
Preparation time: 35 minutes
Cooking time: 40 minutes
Oven temperature: 200°C (400°F), Gas Mark 6, then 180°C (350°F), Gas Mark 4

Smoked Salmon and Potato Tart

750 g/1½ lb boiled potatoes, cooled
65 g/2½ oz butter, melted
250 g/8 oz cream cheese, softened
2 tablespoons chopped fresh dill
1 tablespoon lemon juice
1 egg, beaten
125 g/4 oz smoked salmon, cut in strips
2 tablespoons grated mature Cheddar
  cheese
salt and pepper

1 Slice the potatoes very thinly. Grease a 23 cm/9 inch tart tin with a little of the melted butter. Set aside one-third of the potatoes. Arrange the rest in overlapping slices over the base and sides of the tin, brushing each slice lightly with melted butter and sprinkling salt and pepper between the layers.

2 In a bowl, beat together the cream cheese, dill, lemon juice and egg, with salt and pepper to taste. Spread half the mixture over the potato case and sprinkle with the smoked salmon. Spread the rest of the cream cheese mixture over the salmon.

3 Top with the reserved potato slices, brush with butter and season as before until the filling is covered. Sprinkle with cheese and bake at 200°C (400°F), Gas Mark 6 for 35-40 minutes, until the top is brown and crisp.

Serves 6
Preparation time: 30 minutes
Cooking time: 35-40 minutes
Oven temperature: 200°C (400°F),
Gas Mark 6

Quiche Lorraine

PASTRY:
175 g/6 oz plain flour
75 g/3 oz chilled butter, diced

FILLING:
175 g/6 oz thin asparagus spears
5 eggs
150 ml/¼ pint single cream
25 g/1 oz grated Parmesan cheese
salt and pepper

1 Measure the flour into a bowl. Add the butter and rub in with the fingertips until the mixture resembles fine breadcrumbs. Add the egg yolk and enough cold water, about 1-2 tablespoons, to mix to a firm dough. Cover and chill for 30 minutes, if time permits.
2 Roll out the dough on a lightly floured surface and use to line a 23 cm/9 inch flan tin. Chill the pastry case for 30 minutes. Fill with crumpled foil and bake in a preheated oven, 200°C (400°F), Gas Mark 6 for 15 minutes. Remove the foil and bake for a further 10 minutes. Lower the oven temperature to 180°C (350°F), Gas Mark 4.
3 Make the filling. Grill the bacon until crisp, then drain on paper towels; crumble or cut into pieces. Beat the cream and eggs in a bowl with grated nutmeg, salt and pepper to taste. Sprinkle the bacon over the flan case and pour the cream and egg filling over the top.
4 Place the flan tin on a baking sheet and bake for 30-35 minutes, until the filling is just set and the pastry is golden brown. Serve the quiche warm or cold.

Serves 4-6
Preparation time: 20 minutes, plus chilling time
Cooking time: 55-60 minutes
Oven temperature: 200°C (400°F), Gas Mark 6; then 180°C (350°F), Gas Mark 4

VARIATIONS

Asparagus Tart

Replace the bacon with 250 g/8 oz cooked fresh or drained canned asparagus spears and proceed as in the main recipe.

Mushroom Tart

Melt 25 g/1 oz butter in a frying pan and cook 250 g/8 oz sliced mushrooms until softened. Spread the mushrooms over the flan case instead of the bacon and proceed as in the main recipe.

Roasted Vegetable and Feta Tart

PASTRY:

125 g/4 oz self-raising flour
50 g/2 oz oatmeal
75 g/3 oz chilled butter, diced

FILLING:

1 aubergine, sliced
1 red pepper, cored, seeded and cut
 into thick strips
1 onion, cut into wedges
2 courgettes, cut into sticks
3 tomatoes, halved
2 garlic cloves, chopped
3 tablespoons olive oil
2 teaspoons chopped fresh rosemary
125 g/4 oz feta cheese, crumbled
2 tablespoons grated Parmesan cheese
salt and pepper

1 Mix the flour and oatmeal in a bowl. Add the butter and rub in with the fingertips. Add cold water, about 2-3 tablespoons, to mix to a firm dough. Turn out on to a lightly floured surface and knead briefly.
2 Roll out the pastry and line a 23 cm/9 inch pie plate. Fill with crumpled foil and bake in a preheated oven, 200°C (400°F), Gas Mark 6 for 15 minutes, then remove the foil and return the pastry case to the oven for 5 minutes.
3 Meanwhile, cook the filling. Mix all the vegetables in a roasting tin. Add the garlic, oil and rosemary and season to taste. Turn the mixture over several times to coat the vegetables evenly. Roast at 200°C (400°F), Gas Mark 6 for 35 minutes until the vegetables are tender.
4 Fill the pastry case with the cooked vegetables, scatter the feta cheese over the top and sprinkle with the Parmesan. Return the tart to the oven for 10 minutes. Serve warm or cold.

Serves 6
Preparation time: 25 minutes
Cooking time: 50-55 minutes
Oven temperature: 200°C (400°F),
Gas Mark 6

Aubergine, Tomato and Haloumi Cheese Tart

Haloumi is a creamy-textured, slightly sharp tasting Greek cheese which goes particularly well with aubergine. If you can't find haloumi use mozzarella cheese instead.

250 g/8 oz puff pastry, thawed if frozen
beaten egg or milk, to glaze
1 tablespoon sun-dried tomato paste
375 g/12 oz aubergines, sliced
2 tablespoons olive oil
5 ripe tomatoes, sliced
125 g/4 oz haloumi cheese, sliced thinly
2 teaspoons chopped fresh oregano
50 g/2 oz green olives, stoned and halved
salt and pepper

1 Roll out the pastry on a lightly floured surface to a 25 cm/10 inch square. Place the pastry on a greased baking sheet. Using a sharp pointed knife, make 2 L-shaped cuts in the pastry 2.5 cm/1 inch in from the edges, leaving the 2 opposite corners uncut. Brush the edges of the pastry with water.

2 Lift up one cut corner and draw it across the pastry to the opposite cut side. Repeat with the other cut side to form a pastry case. Brush the edges of the pastry with egg or milk and prick the base. Spread the sun-dried tomato paste over the base of the pastry case.

3 Place the aubergine slices on a grill pan and brush with oil. Cook under a preheated moderate grill until lightly browned, then turn the aubergine slices over, brush again with oil and brown on the other side.

4 Arrange the aubergine slices, tomatoes and cheese in the pastry case. Sprinkle with oregano and olives and add salt and pepper to taste. Bake in a preheated oven, 200°C (400°F), Gas Mark 6 for 25 minutes, until the pastry is golden and the filling tender. Serve warm.

Serves 4
Preparation time: 20 minutes
Cooking time: 25 minutes
Oven temperature: 200°C (400°F), Gas Mark 6

Asparagus, Parmesan and Egg Tart

This tart makes good use of a small amount of asparagus, so make it when this luxury vegetable is in season and at its best. The thin spears are the ones to choose.

PASTRY:
175 g/6 oz plain flour
75 g/3 oz chilled butter, diced

FILLING:
175 g/6 oz thin asparagus spears
5 eggs
150 ml/¼ pint single cream
25 g/1 oz grated Parmesan cheese
salt and pepper

1 Measure the flour into a bowl, add the butter and rub in with the fingertips until the mixture resembles fine breadcrumbs. Add enough cold water, about 2 tablespoons, to mix to a firm dough. Roll out on a lightly floured surface and line a 20 cm/8 inch flan tin. Chill for 30 minutes, if time permits.

2 Fill the pastry case with crumpled foil and bake in a preheated oven, 200°C (400°F), Gas Mark 6 for 15 minutes, then remove the foil and return the pastry case to the oven for 10 minutes more. Lower the oven temperature to 180°C (350°F), Gas Mark 4.

3 Make the filling. Trim the woody ends from the asparagus. Stand them upright in a tall saucepan. Add salted boiling water to cover all but the tips of the asparagus. Cover the pan with foil or a lid and cook for 7-10 minutes, until tender. Drain the asparagus in a colander and refresh under cold running water. Drain again.

4 Beat one of the eggs in a bowl with the cream. Add salt and pepper to taste. Arrange the asparagus in the base of the flan case. Break each of the 4 remaining eggs in turn into a saucer, and carefully slide them into the flan case. Pour over the cream mixture. Sprinkle with Parmesan.

5 Return the tart to the oven for 15-20 minutes, until the eggs have just set. Serve warm.

Serves 4
Preparation time: 35 minutes.
Cooking time: 40-45 minutes
Oven temperature: 200°C (400°F), Gas Mark 6, then 180°C (350°F), Gas Mark 4

VARIATION

Asparagus and Egg Tartlets

Make up the pastry as in the main recipe and line 4 x 9 cm/3 ½ inch tartlet tins. Bake the pastry cases for 15 minutes only, removing the foil after 10 minutes. Curl the asparagus into each pastry case and crack an egg into each. Divide the cream mixture between the tartlets and sprinkle with Parmesan. Bake the filled tartlets for 15-20 minutes. Serve warm as a starter or snack, or cold for a picnic or in a lunch box.

Mozzarella and Tomato Tartlets

75 g/3 oz butter
1 onion, sliced thinly
150 g/5 oz plain flour
125 g/4 oz mashed potato
375 g/12 oz plum tomatoes, sliced
125 g/4 oz mozzarella cheese, sliced
50 g/2 oz black olives, stoned
few basil leaves, torn into small pieces
salt and pepper

1 Melt 25g/1 oz of the butter in a small frying pan, add the onion and fry for about 5 minutes until softened and lightly browned. Cool. Cut the remaining butter into cubes and rub into the flour in a bowl. Stir in the mashed potato and onion, with the pan juices. Add salt and pepper to taste. Mix to a soft dough.
2 Divide the dough into 4 and press out into 12 cm/5 inch rounds on a greased baking sheet. Pinch the edges of each round to form a rim.
3 Arrange the tomatoes over the top of each to within 1 cm/½ inch of the edge. Arrange the mozzarella over the top and sprinkle with the olives.
4 Bake in a preheated oven, 200°C (400°F), Gas Mark 6 for 25-30 minutes until the cheese topping is golden. Sprinkle the tartlets with the torn basil leaves and serve hot.

Serves 4
Preparation time: 25 minutes
Cooking time: 25-30 minutes
Oven temperature: 200°C (400°F), Gas Mark 6

Cheshire Cheese and Leek Tart

PASTRY:
125 g/4 oz self-raising flour
50 g/2 oz oatmeal
75 g/3 oz chilled butter, diced

FILLING:
2 garlic cloves, chopped
3 tablespoons olive oil
3 leeks, trimmed, cleaned and sliced
2 teaspoons chopped fresh rosemary
2 eggs, beaten
150 ml/¼ pint milk
125 g/4 oz Cheshire cheese, crumbled
2 tablespoons grated Parmesan cheese
salt and pepper

1 Mix the flour and oatmeal in a bowl. Add the butter and rub in with the fingertips until the mixture resembles breadcrumbs. Add enough cold water, about 2-3 tablespoons, to mix to a firm dough. Turn the dough out on to a lightly floured surface and knead briefly.
2 Roll out the pastry and line a 23 cm/9 inch pie plate. Make cuts around the pastry rim at 2.5 cm/ 1 inch intervals, brush the rim with water, then fold every other piece of pastry upwards and seal. Fill with crumpled foil and bake in a preheated oven 200°C (400°F), Gas Mark 6 for 15 minutes, then remove foil and return the pastry case to the oven for 5 minutes. Set the pastry case aside. Lower the oven temperature to 180°C (350°F), Gas Mark 4.
3 Make the filling. Soften the chopped garlic in the oil in a frying pan over a moderate heat, then add the sliced leeks and cook gently for 7-10 minutes, until softened. Stir in the rosemary, with salt and pepper to taste, then spread the filling over the flan case.
4 Beat the eggs, milk and Cheshire cheese in a bowl; pour into the pastry case over the filling. Sprinkle with Parmesan cheese and bake for 30-35 minutes, until the filling is set and golden brown. Serve the tart warm or cold.

Serves 6
Preparation time: 25 minutes
Cooking time: 50-55 minutes
Oven temperature: 200°C (400°F), Gas Mark 6, then 180°C (350°F), Gas Mark 4

Wild Mushrooms in Crispy Bread Cases

BREAD CASES:
8 thin slices bread, crusts removed
50 g/2 oz butter, melted
FILLING:
25 g/1 oz butter
1 shallot, chopped
175 g/6 oz mushrooms, (chestnut,
    oyster, shiitake) sliced

1 tablespoon Madeira
4 tablespoons double cream
1 tablespoon chopped fresh parsley
salt and pepper
assorted salad leaves, to serve

1 Brush both sides of the bread with the butter. Press firmly into 8 tartlet or bun tins. Bake in a preheated oven, 200°C (400°F), Gas Mark 6 for 10-15 minutes, until crisp and golden brown.
2 Meanwhile, make the filling. Melt the butter in a small saucepan, add the shallot and fry for about 5 minutes until softened. Add the mushrooms and cook for a further 5 minutes, until tender. Stir in the Madeira and allow to bubble briefly, then stir in the cream and chopped parsley, with salt and pepper to taste. Cook over a moderate heat for a few minutes, until the mixture forms a sauce.
3 Arrange the salad leaves on 8 small plates and place a bread case on each. Fill with the mushroom mixture and serve warm.

Serves 8
Preparation time: 15 minutes
Cooking time: 10-15 minutes
Oven temperature: 200°C (400°F), Gas Mark 6

Chicken, Celery and Bacon Tartlets

8 bread cases, see main recipe
FILLING:
25 g/1 oz butter
1 celery stick, sliced
2 rindless smoked back bacon
    rashers, chopped
125 g/4 oz skinless chicken breast,
    chopped
1 tablespoon sherry
3 tablespoons double cream
1 tablespoon chopped fresh parsley
salt and pepper

Prepare the bread cases and filling as in the main recipe, substituting the celery for the shallot and using the bacon and chicken instead of the mushrooms. Use sherry in place of Madeira and finish as in main recipe.

Smoked Haddock and Spinach Tart

Smoked haddock gives this simple tart a delicious savoury flavour. Serve it for supper with new potatoes and a chicory and orange salad.

PASTRY:
75 g/3 oz wholemeal flour
75 g/3 oz plain flour
75 g/3 oz chilled butter, diced
FILLING:
350 g/12 oz smoked haddock fillet
300 ml/½ pint milk
125 g/4 oz frozen leaf spinach, thawed
40 g/1½ oz butter
25 g/1 oz plain flour
2 eggs, beaten
75 g/3 oz mature Cheddar cheese, grated
salt and pepper

1 Mix the flours in a bowl. Add the butter and rub in with the fingertips until the mixture resembles fine breadcrumbs. Stir in enough cold water, about 2-3 tablespoons, to mix to a firm dough.
2 Knead dough briefly on a lightly floured surface, then roll out and line a 20 cm/8 inch deep flan tin. Fill with crumpled foil and bake in a preheated oven, 200°C (400°F), Gas Mark 6 for 15 minutes. Remove the flan case, discard the foil and lower the oven temperature to 190°C (375°F), Gas Mark 5.

3 Make the filling. Place the haddock in a pan and pour over the milk. Bring to the boil, then cover the pan, lower the heat and cook gently for about 10 minutes, until the haddock is tender and flakes easily when tested with the tip of a knife. Using a slotted spoon, remove the fish from the pan. Strain the cooking liquid into a jug. Skin and flake the fish.
4 Press the spinach in a sieve to extract as much liquid as possible. Heat the butter in a pan until bubbling, stir in the flour and cook for 1 minute. Gradually stir in the cooking liquid from the fish, stirring until the sauce is thick and smooth.

5 Cool the sauce for 5 minutes, then stir in the spinach, eggs and haddock. Add 50 g/2 oz of the cheese, with salt and pepper to taste. Stir well, then pour into the flan case.
6 Sprinkle with the remaining cheese and bake for about 25 minutes, until the filling is risen and golden brown. Serve warm.

Serves 4-6
Preparation time: 20 minutes
Cooking time: 40 minutes
Oven temperature: 200°C (400°F), Gas Mark 6, then 190°C (375°F), Gas Mark 5

Grilled Pepper and Onion Tart

YEAST PASTRY:

125 g/4 oz strong white flour
125 g/4 oz strong wholemeal flour
1 teaspoon easy-blend yeast
1 teaspoon salt
150 ml/¼ pint hand-hot water
1 tablespoon olive oil

TOPPING:

1 x 250 g/8 oz can chopped tomatoes
1 tablespoon tomato purée
2 teaspoons dried oregano
1 onion, cut into wedges
2 red peppers, cored, seeded and cut
   into strips
2 yellow peppers, cored, seeded and
   cut into strips
2 tablespoons olive oil
salt and pepper

1 Mix the flours, yeast and salt in a bowl. Add the water and oil and mix quickly to a soft dough. Turn the dough out on to a lightly floured surface and knead for 5 minutes. Place the dough in a large oiled polythene bag, tie the top loosely and leave to rise for 30 minutes.

2 Make the topping. Combine the chopped tomatoes and tomato purée in a saucepan. Add 1 teaspoon of the oregano, with salt and pepper to taste. Bring to the boil, stirring, then lower the heat and simmer for about 5 minutes, until thickened. Leave to cool.

3 Place the onion wedges and peppers on a sheet of oiled foil on a grill rack. Brush with oil, sprinkle with salt and pepper. Cook under a preheated hot grill for about 10 minutes, turning frequently, until softened and slightly charred.

4 Roll out the pastry on a lightly floured surface to a 25 cm/10 inch square and place on a greased baking sheet. Fold up the edges of the pastry to form a rim. Spread with the tomato topping, then arrange the chargrilled peppers and onion over the top. Sprinkle with the remaining oregano.

5 Bake the tart in a preheated oven, 220°C (425°F), Gas Mark 7 for 20-25 minutes, until the pastry edges are crisp and golden brown. Serve the tart warm.

Serves 4-6
Preparation time: 45 minutes
Cooking time: 20-25 minutes
Oven temperature: 220°C (425°F), Gas Mark 7

Onion, Raisin and Pine Nut Tart

75 g/3 oz butter
2 teaspoons mustard seeds
150 g/5 oz plain flour
125 g/4 oz mashed potato
2 tablespoons olive oil

2 onions, sliced thinly
125 g/4 oz mozzarella cheese, sliced
25 g/1 oz pine nuts
25 g/1 oz raisins
salt and pepper

1 Heat 25 g/1 oz of the butter in a small frying pan. Fry the mustard seeds until they start to pop. Cube the remaining butter, then rub it into the flour in a mixing bowl. Stir in the mashed potato and the mustard seeds with the melted butter. Add salt and pepper to taste and mix to a soft dough.
2 Press the dough out on to a greased baking sheet to a 25 cm/10 inch square. Pinch the edges to make a rim.
3 Heat the oil in a frying pan, add the onions and fry for about 5 minutes until soft and lightly browned. Arrange the mozzarella slices evenly over the pastry base, then scatter the pine nuts and raisins over the top. Cover with the onions and sprinkle with salt and pepper.
4 Bake in a preheated oven, 200°C (400°F), Gas Mark 6 for 25-30 minutes, until the pastry is golden brown. Serve hot.

Serves 4
Preparation time: 25 minutes
Cooking time: 25-30 minutes
Oven temperature: 200°C (400°F), Gas Mark 6

VARIATION

Tomato and Mozzarella Tart

75 g/3 oz butter
1 onion, sliced thinly
150 g/5 oz plain flour
125 g/4 oz mashed potato
375 g/12 oz plum tomatoes
125 g/4 oz mozzarella cheese, sliced
50 g/2 oz black olives, stoned
few basil leaves, torn into small pieces
salt and pepper

1 Melt 25 g/1 oz of the butter in a small frying pan, add the onion and fry for about 5 minutes until softened and lightly browned. Cool. Cube the remaining butter and rub it into the flour in a bowl. Stir in the mashed potato and onion, with the pan juices. Add salt and pepper to taste. Mix to a soft dough.
2 Press dough out to a 23 cm/ 9 inch round on a greased baking sheet. Pinch the edges to form a rim. Arrange the tomatoes over the top to within 1 cm/½ inch of the edge. Arrange the mozzarella over the top and sprinkle with the olives.
3 Bake as in main recipe. Sprinkle with the torn basil leaves and serve hot.

1 Measure the flour into a bowl, add the butter and rub in with the fingertips until the mixture resembles fine breadcrumbs. Stir in the cheese, mustard and egg yolk, with enough water, about 1 tablespoon, to mix to a firm dough.

2 Knead the dough briefly on a lightly floured surface, then roll out and line a 23 cm/9 inch flan tin. Chill for 30 minutes, if time permits, then fill with crumpled foil and bake in a preheated oven, 200°C (400°F), Gas Mark 6 for about 20 minutes, removing the foil for the last 5 minutes.

3 Make the filling. Layer the sliced ripe tomatoes and torn basil leaves in the flan case, sprinkling each layer with salt and pepper. Arrange the cherry tomatoes and sun-dried tomatoes over the top.

4 Heat the oil in a small frying pan, add the garlic and fry briefly until it starts to colour. Dribble the garlic mixture over the filling, then sprinkle with Parmesan. Return the tart to the oven for 15 minutes, until the tomatoes are softened and the top browned. Serve warm.

Serves 6
Preparation time: 20 minutes
Cooking time: 35 minutes
Oven temperature: 200°C (400°F), Gas Mark 6

Three Tomato and Basil Tart

PASTRY:
175 g/6 oz plain flour
75 g/3 oz chilled butter, diced
25 g/1 oz grated Parmesan cheese
1 teaspoon wholegrain mustard
1 egg yolk

FILLING:
375 g/12 oz ripe tomatoes, sliced
handful torn basil leaves
125 g/4 oz cherry tomatoes, halved
50 g/2 oz sun-dried tomatoes, sliced
1 tablespoon olive oil
2 garlic cloves, sliced
1 tablespoon grated Parmesan cheese
salt and pepper
basil leaves, to garnish

Prawn and Courgette Tart

PASTRY:

150 g/6 oz plain flour
75 g/3 oz chilled butter, diced

FILLING:

40 g/1½ oz butter
1 courgette, cut into matchsticks
25 g/1 oz plain flour
300 ml/½ pint hot milk
175 g/6 oz peeled cooked prawns,
   thawed if frozen
2 eggs, beaten
75 g/3 oz mature Cheddar cheese,
   grated
salt and pepper

1 Measure the flour into a bowl. Add the diced butter and rub in with the fingertips until the mixture resembles fine breadcrumbs. Stir in enough cold water, about 2-3 tablespoons, to mix to a firm dough.
2 Knead the dough briefly on a lightly floured surface, then roll out and line a 20 cm/8 inch square flan tin. Fill with crumpled foil and bake in a preheated oven, 200°C (400°F), Gas Mark 6 for 15 minutes. Remove the flan case from the oven, discard the foil and lower the oven temperature to 190°C (375°F), Gas Mark 5.
3 Make the filling. Melt the butter in a saucepan, add the courgette matchsticks and cook gently for about 5 minutes until softened. Stir in the flour and cook for 1 minute.

Gradually stir in the hot milk, cooking until the sauce is thick and smooth.
4 Cool the sauce slightly, then stir in the prawns and eggs with 50 g/ 2 oz of the grated cheese. Add salt and pepper to taste. Pour the filling into the flan case and sprinkle with the remaining grated cheese.
5 Bake for about 25 minutes, until the filling is risen and golden brown. Serve warm.

Serves 4-6
Preparation time: 25 minutes
Cooking time: 40 minutes
Oven temperature: 200°C (400°F), Gas Mark 6, then 190°C (375°F), Gas Mark 5

Leek and Mussel Tart

Fish counters now sell mussels ready cooked, but if you prefer to buy them raw you will need about 500 g/1 lb. Scrub them thoroughly and place in a pan with a little water or wine. Cook over a high heat, shaking the pan until the shells open. Discard any that remain shut.

PASTRY:

175 g/6 oz plain flour

75 g/3 oz chilled butter, diced

1 egg yolk

FILLING:

25 g/1 oz butter

2 leeks, trimmed, cleaned and sliced

175 g/6 oz shelled cooked mussels

3 tablespoons crème fraîche

2 tablespoons dried breadcrumbs

3 tablespoons chopped fresh parsley

1 garlic clove, chopped

2 tablespoons olive oil

salt and pepper

1 Measure the flour into a bowl, add the butter and rub in with the fingertips until the mixture resembles fine breadcrumbs. Stir in the egg yolk and enough cold water, about 1 tablespoon, to mix to a firm dough.

2 Knead the dough briefly on a lightly floured surface, then roll out and line a 20 cm/8 inch flan tin. Chill for 30 minutes, if time permits, then fill the pastry case with crumpled foil and bake in a preheated oven 200°C (400°F), Gas Mark 6 for 25 minutes. Remove the foil for the last 10 minutes to allow the pastry to brown.

3 Meanwhile, make the filling. Melt the butter in a saucepan, add the leeks and fry gently for about 5 minutes until softened and tender. Add the mussels and crème fraîche, with salt and pepper to taste. Stir over a gentle heat until warmed through.

4 Mix the breadcrumbs, parsley, garlic and oil in a small bowl. Fill the warm pastry case with the mussel and leek mixture then sprinkle the crumb mixture over the top. Place under a preheated moderate grill until the crumbs are browned and crisp. Serve warm.

Serves 4-6

Preparation time: 25 minutes

Cooking time: 30 minutes

Oven temperature: 200°C (400°F), Gas Mark 6

Plum Tomato and Anchovy Tart

PASTRY:
175 g/6 oz plain flour
75 g/3 oz chilled butter, diced
FILLING:
750 g/1½ lb plum tomatoes
1 tablespoon olive oil
1 tablespoon tomato purée
1 garlic clove, crushed
2 tablespoons chopped celery leaves
pinch of sugar
1 x 50 g/2 oz can anchovies, drained and halved lengthways
25 g/1 oz capers
salt and pepper

1 Measure the flour into a bowl. Add the butter and rub in with the fingertips until the mixture resembles fine breadcrumbs. Add enough cold water, about 2-3 tablespoons, to mix to a firm dough.
2 Turn the dough out on to a lightly floured surface and knead briefly. Roll out and line a 20 cm/8 inch square or 23 cm/9 inch round flan tin. Chill the pastry case for 30 minutes, if time permits.
3 Fill the pastry case with crumpled foil and bake in a preheated oven, 200°C (400°F), Gas Mark 6 for 15 minutes, then remove the foil and bake for 10 minutes more until the pastry case is cooked.
4 Make the filling. Place the plum tomatoes in a bowl and pour over boiling water to cover. Leave for

1-2 minutes, then drain. Cut a cross in the stem end of each tomato and remove the skins. Quarter the skinned tomatoes and remove the seeds. Place the tomatoes in a pan with the olive oil, tomato purée, garlic and chopped celery leaves. Sprinkle with the sugar and add salt and pepper to taste. Bring to the boil, lower the heat and simmer for 15-20 minutes, until the tomato sauce is thick and pulpy.

5 Spread the tomato sauce over the pastry case. Arrange the anchovies on top in a criss-cross pattern. Sprinkle with the capers, then return the tart to the oven for 10 minutes to heat through. Serve.

Serves 4
Preparation time: 30 minutes
Cooking time: 35 minutes
Oven temperature: 200°C (400°F), Gas Mark 6

boiling water with the lemon juice. Cover and cook for 10 minutes, until the chicory is just tender, drain well.
4 Cut each chicory head in half lengthways and wrap each piece in a slice of ham. Arrange in the pastry case radiating from the centre. Beat together the eggs, cream, Parmesan and seasoning then pour into the pastry case.
5 Bake the tart for 25-30 minutes, until the filling is firm and golden brown. Serve warm.

Serves 4-6

Preparation time: 25 minutes
Cooking time: 35-40 minutes
Oven temperature: 200°C (400°F), Gas Mark 6, then 180°C (350°F), Gas Mark 4

Chicory and Ham Tart

PASTRY:

125 g/4 oz plain flour
50 g/2 oz oatmeal
75 g/3 oz butter, diced

FILLING:

3 small heads chicory
2 tablespoons lemon juice
6 slices parma ham or cooked ham
2 eggs
150 ml/¼ pint single cream
25 g/1 oz grated Parmesan cheese
salt and pepper

1 Mix together the flour and oatmeal in a bowl. Add the butter and rub in with the fingertips until the mixture resembles fine breadcrumbs. Add 3-4 tablespoons cold water and mix to a firm dough.
2 Knead briefly on a lightly floured surface, then roll out and line a 20 cm/8 inch flan tin. Line with crumpled foil and bake in a preheated oven, 200°C (400°F) Gas Mark 6 for 10 minutes. Remove the flan case and reduce the oven temperature to 180°C (350°F), Gas Mark 4.
3 Add the chicory to a saucepan of

Potato Tart with Ham, Artichokes and Mushrooms

This free-form tart has a moist scone-like dough which is perfect for all sorts of savoury toppings.

75 g/3 oz butter
1 onion, sliced thinly
150 g/5 oz plain flour
125 g/4 oz mashed potato
1 tablespoon olive oil
2 shallots, sliced

125 g/4 oz mushrooms, sliced
125 g/4 oz cooked ham, cut into strips
175 g/6 oz drained canned artichoke
    hearts, sliced
salt and pepper

1 Melt 25 g/1 oz of the butter in a small saucepan, add the onion and fry for about 5 minutes, until softened and lightly browned. Cool slightly.
2 Dice the remaining butter and rub it into the flour in a mixing bowl. Add the onion with the pan juices, the mashed potato and salt and pepper to taste. Mix to a soft dough.
3 Press the dough out on a greased baking sheet to a 23 cm/9 inch round. Pinch the edges of the dough to make a rim.
4 Heat the oil in a frying pan, add the shallots and fry until lightly browned. Add the mushrooms and cook briefly until softened.
5 Scatter the ham and artichokes over the dough, then top with the shallots and mushroom mixture. Season with salt and pepper and bake in a preheated oven, 200°C (400°F), Gas Mark 6 for 25-30 minutes, until the pastry is golden brown. Serve hot.

Serves 4
Preparation time: 20 minutes
Cooking time: 25-30 minutes
Oven temperature: 200°C (400°F), Gas Mark 6

SWEET PIES

Mango Star Pie

500 g/1 lb puff pastry, thawed if frozen
2 ripe mangoes
2 tablespoons lime juice
50 g/2 oz creamed coconut, grated
25 g/1 oz demerara sugar
beaten egg and caster sugar, to glaze

1 Roll out half the pastry to a 30 cm/12 inch round. Make V-shaped cuts all round to form a star shape. Roll out the remaining pastry to a 30 cm/12 inch round and place the star-shaped pastry on top. Using a sharp knife cut the lower piece of pastry to a star shape, using the upper piece as a template.
2 Peel, halve and stone the mangoes. Cut them into thin slices. Place one piece of pastry on a greased baking sheet and arrange the mango slices on top to within 1 cm/½ inch of the edges. Sprinkle with lime juice, coconut and demerara sugar. Brush the edges of the pastry with water and cover with the remaining piece of pastry. Press the edges firmly to seal.
3 Brush the top of the pie with egg and sprinkle with sugar. Bake in a preheated oven, 220°C (425°F), Gas Mark 7 for 20-25 minutes, until risen and golden brown. Serve hot.

Serves 6
Preparation time: 20 minutes
Cooking time: 20-25 minutes
Oven temperature: 220°C (425°F), Gas Mark 7

Gâteau Pithiviers

This delicious pastry cake originated in Pithiviers in France. It is traditionally served on Twelfth Night when it is called 'Tarte de Roi'.

150 g/5 oz unsalted butter, softened
150 g/5 oz icing sugar
2 eggs, beaten
2 tablespoons rum
150 g/5 oz ground almonds
few drops almond essence
500 g/1 lb puff pastry, thawed if
  frozen
TO GLAZE:
1 egg, beaten
50 g/2 oz icing sugar

1 Beat the butter in a bowl until creamy. Beat in the icing sugar, then beat for about 5 minutes more, until light and fluffy. Beat in the eggs, a little at a time, then stir in the rum, ground almonds and essence.
2 Roll out half the pastry and trim to a 28 cm/11 inch round, using a plate as a guide. Place on a greased baking sheet. Spread the filling over the pastry to within 1 cm/½ inch of the edge. Brush the edge with water.
3 Roll out the remaining pastry to a slightly larger round and cover the pie. Press the edges firmly to seal, then trim the edges and flute with the back of a knife. With the point of a sharp knife, score the top of the dough from the centre outwards to represent the spokes of a wheel. Do not cut right through to the filling.
4 Brush the top of the pastry with egg, taking care not to brush the sides, as this will stop the dough from rising. Bake in a preheated oven, 220°C (425°F), Gas Mark 7 for 30 minutes, then remove from the oven and dust with icing sugar. Bake the gâteau for a further 7-10 minutes. Serve warm.

Serves 8-10
Preparation time: 20 minutes
Cooking time: 40 minutes
Oven temperature: 220°C (425°F),
Gas Mark 7

Crunchy Banana and Pineapple Pie

175 g/6 oz ginger biscuits
75 g/3 oz butter, melted
1 banana
200 g/7 oz pineapple chunks, drained
if using canned pineapple
375 g/12 oz medium-fat soft cheese
75 g/3 oz caster sugar
1 teaspoon vanilla essence

1 Crumb the biscuits in a food processor. Alternatively, place them between 2 large sheets of grease-proof paper and crush with a rolling pin. Melt the butter in a saucepan, add the crumbs and stir well. Place 3 tablespoons of the crumb mixture in a small ovenproof dish. Press the remainder over the base and sides of a buttered 20 cm/8 inch pie plate.
2 Bake the pie case and crumbs in a preheated oven, 200°C (400°F), Gas Mark 6 for 10 minutes until crisp, then leave to cool. Mash the banana with half the pineapple, then mix in the cheese, sugar and vanilla. Spread over the pie case. Pile the reserved pineapple on top and sprinkle with the baked crumbs. Chill until ready to serve.

Serves 6-8
Preparation time: 15 minutes
Cooking time: 10 minutes
Oven temperature: 200°C (400°F), Gas Mark 6

Rhubarb and Ginger Pie

375 g/12 oz plain flour
175 g/6 oz chilled butter, diced
125 g/4 oz caster sugar
2 teaspoons grated orange rind
1 egg, beaten
750 g/1½ lb rhubarb, sliced

3 tablespoons orange juice
2 teaspoons ground ginger
TO GLAZE:
milk
caster sugar,

1 Place the flour in a bowl, add the butter and rub in with the fingertips until the mixture resembles fine breadcrumbs. Stir in half the sugar and the orange rind, then add the egg and enough cold water, about 2-3 tablespoons, to mix to a firm dough.
2 Mix the rhubarb, orange juice, ginger and remaining sugar in a bowl. Knead the pastry briefly on a lightly floured surface, then roll out just over half the pastry and line a 23 cm/9 inch pie plate.
3 Fill the pastry case with the rhubarb mixture. Brush the edges of the pastry lightly with water. Roll out the remaining pastry and cover the pie. Trim the edges of the pastry, then pinch the edges to seal. Roll out the pastry trimmings and cut into leaves. Stick to the pie with a little water.
4 Brush the top of the pie with milk and sprinkle with caster sugar. Bake in a preheated oven, 190°C (375°F), Gas Mark 5 for 40-45 minutes, until the pastry is crisp and golden brown. Serve warm.

Serves 6
Preparation time: 20 minutes
Cooking time: 40-45 minutes
Oven temperature: 190°C (375°F), Gas Mark 5

VARIATION

Pineapple and Ginger Pie

Replace the rhubarb with 1 large pineapple, peeled, cored and cut into chunks. Continue as in the main recipe.

Toffee Apple Pie

50 g/2 oz butter

750 g/1½ lb eating apples, peeled, cored and sliced

50 g/2 oz light muscovado sugar

juice of 2 oranges

2 tablespoons brandy or Calvados

375 g/12 oz puff pastry, thawed if frozen

beaten egg, to glaze

1 Melt the butter in a frying pan, add apples and fry all over for about 10 minutes, until just starting to brown. Stir in the sugar, orange juice and brandy and allow the mixture to bubble for a few minutes, until it forms a thick syrup. Remove from the heat and leave to cool.

2 Roll out half the pastry on a lightly floured surface and line a 23 cm/ 9 inch flan tin. Fill with apple mixture and brush pastry edges with water. Roll out remaining pastry and cover pie. Pinch edges together to seal. If liked, mark a zig zag pattern on top of the pie with a knife taking care not to cut through the pastry.

3 Brush with egg. Bake in a preheated oven, 220°C (425°F), Gas Mark 7 for 25-30 minutes, until golden.

Serves 6

Preparation time: 20 minutes

Cooking time: 25-30 minutes

Oven temperature: 220°C (425°F), Gas Mark 7

Alaska Crumble Pie

CRUMB CASE:

175 g/6 oz oat biscuits
75 g/3 oz butter

FILLING:

3 egg whites
175 g/6 oz caster sugar
125 g/4 oz raspberries
125 g/4 oz redcurrants
500 ml/17 fl oz tub vanilla ice cream

1 Crumb the biscuits in a food processor. Alternatively, place them between 2 sheets of greaseproof paper and crush with a rolling pin. Melt the butter in a pan, add the crumbs and stir well. Press mixture evenly over the base and sides of a 23 cm/9 inch pie plate or flan tin and chill until ready to serve.
2 Whisk the egg whites in a grease-free bowl until stiff and dry. Whisk in 1 tablespoon of the sugar, then fold in the remainder.
3 When ready to serve, fill the crumb case with fruit and add scoops of ice cream. Spread the meringue over the top, covering the filling completely. Bake in a preheated oven, 200°C (400°F), Gas Mark 6 for 5-8 minutes, until the meringue is golden. Serve immediately.

Serves 4-6
Preparation time: 15 minutes
Cooking time: 5-8 minutes
Oven temperature: 200°C (400°F), Gas Mark 6

Peach and Honey Pie

PASTRY:
250 g/8 oz plain flour
125 g/4 oz chilled butter, diced
50 g/2 oz ground hazelnuts
25 g/1 oz caster sugar

FILLING:
6 ripe peaches, stoned and sliced
2 tablespoons clear honey
25 g/1 oz shelled hazelnuts
3 cardamom pods
beaten egg or milk, to glaze
sugar, see method

1 Place the flour in a bowl. Add the butter and rub in with the fingertips until the mixture resembles fine breadcrumbs. Stir in the hazelnuts and sugar, then add enough cold water, about 3-4 tablespoons, to mix to a firm dough.
2 Turn the dough out on to a lightly floured surface and knead briefly. Roll out two-thirds of the dough and line a 23 cm/9 inch pie plate. Wrap the remaining dough closely and set it aside.
3 Pile the peaches into the pastry case. Drizzle over the honey and sprinkle with the hazelnuts. Split the cardamom pods and scrape out the seeds. Sprinkle the seeds over the filling.
4 Roll out the remaining dough and cut into 2.5 cm/1 inch wide strips. Brush the edge of the pie with water. Arrange the strips in a lattice design over the pie, with a little of the filling showing.
5 Brush the pastry with egg or milk and sprinkle with sugar. Bake in a preheated oven, 200°C (400°F), Gas Mark 6 for 35-40 minutes, until the pastry is golden brown. Serve warm or cold.

Serve 6
Preparation time: 25 minutes
Cooking time: 35-40 minutes
Oven temperature: 200°C (400°F), Gas Mark 6

Apple and Raisin Dumplings

PASTRY:
250 g/8 oz plain flour
125 g/4 oz chilled butter, diced
25 g/1 oz caster sugar
1 egg yolk

FILLING:
4 cooking apples
1 tablespoon lemon juice
25 g/1 oz demerara sugar
25 g/1 oz butter, diced
50 g/2 oz raisins
½ teaspoon mixed spice

TO GLAZE:
1 egg white, lightly beaten
caster sugar

1 Make the filling. Peel and core the apples, then brush them with lemon juice to prevent them discolouring. Mix the demerara sugar, butter, raisins and mixed spice in a bowl and set aside.

2 Make the pastry. Place the flour in a mixing bowl. Add the diced butter and rub in with the fingertips until the mixture resembles fine breadcrumbs. Stir in the caster sugar, then add the egg yolk and enough cold water, about 3-4 tablespoons, to mix to a firm dough.

3 Turn the dough out on to a lightly floured surface and knead briefly. Divide the dough into 4 pieces and roll each to a 15 cm/6 inch square. Place a peeled and cored apple in the centre of each of the squares and fill with the raisin mixture.

4 Brush the edges of each piece of pastry with water, then draw up over the apple to enclose it completely. Place the apple and raisin dumplings on a baking sheet and brush with the lightly beaten egg white. Dredge thickly with caster sugar and bake in a preheated oven, 200°C (400°F), Gas Mark 6 for 40-45 minutes, until the pastry is golden brown. Serve the apple and raisin dumplings hot with cream or custard.

Serves 4
Preparation time: 30 minutes
Cooking time: 40-45 minutes
Oven temperature: 200°C (400°F), Gas Mark 6

Pecan Pie

PASTRY:
250 g/8 oz plain flour
125 g/4 oz chilled butter, diced
25 g/1 oz caster sugar
FILLING:
125 g/4 oz dark muscovado sugar
4 tablespoons molasses
4 tablespoons golden syrup
75 g/3 oz butter, melted
1 teaspoon vanilla essence
grated rind of 1 lemon
4 eggs, beaten
175 g/6 oz pecan halves

1 Make the pastry. Place the flour in a bowl, add the butter and rub in until mixture resembles fine breadcrumbs. Stir in the sugar, then add enough cold water, about 3-4 tablespoons to mix to a firm dough.
2 Knead the dough briefly on a lightly floured surface, then roll out and line a 28 x 18 cm/11 x 7 inch shallow oblong tin. Chill pastry case for 30 minutes, if time permits.
3 Make the filling. Mix the sugar, molasses, syrup, butter and vanilla in a bowl. Stir in the lemon rind and eggs and mix well. Chop half the nuts and add to the filling mixture. Pour into the prepared pastry case.
4 Arrange the remaining pecans over the top of the pie. Bake in a preheated oven, 180°C (350°F), Gas Mark 4 for 45-50 minutes, until the pastry is golden brown and the filling has set. Leave to cool, then cut into squares to serve.

Serves 8-10
Preparation time: 25 minutes
Cooking time: 45-50 minutes
Oven temperature: 180°C (350°F), Gas Mark 4

VARIATIONS

Walnut and Orange Pie

Replace the pecans with walnut halves and use the grated rind of 1 orange instead of the lemon.

Chocolate and Pecan Pie

Add 25 g/1 oz sifted cocoa powder to the filling mixture. Sprinkle 50 g/2 oz grated chocolate over the cooled baked pie.

Mincemeat and Clementine Pie

PASTRY:
75 g/3 oz plain flour
75 g/3 oz wholemeal flour
75 g/3 oz chilled butter, diced
50 g/2 oz ground almonds
25 g/1 oz caster sugar
grated rind of 1 orange
1 egg, beaten

FILLING:
375 g/12 oz luxury mincemeat
3 clementines, peeled and segmented
icing sugar, for dusting

1 Make the pastry. Place the plain and wholemeal flours in a bowl, add the diced butter and rub in with the fingertips until the mixture resembles fine breadcrumbs. Stir in the ground almonds, sugar and orange rind, then add the egg and mix to a firm dough.
2 Knead the dough briefly on a lightly floured surface, then roll out and line a 20 cm/8 inch flan tin. Gather up the pastry trimmings, reroll and cut into holly shapes. Stick some of the holly shapes to the edge of the pastry case with a little water. Reserve about 6 holly shapes. Chill the pastry shell for 30 minutes, if time permits.
3 Mix the mincemeat and clementine segments in a bowl; spread the mixture over the pastry case. Arrange the reserved holly shapes over the top. Bake in a preheated oven, 200°C (400°F), Gas Mark 6 for 25-30 minutes, until the pastry is golden brown. Dust with icing sugar and serve warm or cold.

Serves 6
Preparation time: 20 minutes
Cooking time: 25-30 minutes
Oven temperature: 200°C (400°F), Gas Mark 6

VARIATIONS

Cranberry and Mincemeat Pie

Make and bake the pie as in the main recipe, replacing the clementines with 175 g/6 oz fresh or frozen cranberries.

Rich Mince Pies

Make the pastry as in main recipe using 250 g/8 oz plain flour and omitting the wholemeal flour. Add 2-3 tablespoons orange juice. Knead the dough briefly on a lightly floured surface. Roll out thinly and stamp out 12 x 7.5 cm/3 inch rounds. Line 12 bun tins with the pastry, pressing the rounds into the tins. Fill with 250 g/8 oz mincemeat. Roll out the remaining pastry and cut into 5 cm/2 inch rounds to cover pies. Brush with egg white and dredge with caster sugar. Bake as in main recipe for about 20 minutes until golden. Serve warm.

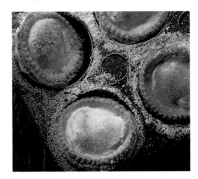

Pumpkin Pie

To make pumpkin purée, simply steam or boil pumpkin chunks for 15-20 minutes until tender, then drain thoroughly. Purée in a blender or food processor or press through a sieve.

PASTRY:
250 g/8 oz plain flour
125 g/4 oz chilled butter, diced
25 g/1 oz caster sugar
FILLING:
250 g/8 oz pumpkin purée or
   1 x 475 g/15 oz can pumpkin pureé
2 eggs, beaten
150 ml/¼ pint single cream
75 g/3 oz dark muscovado sugar
1 teaspoon ground cinnamon
½ teaspoon ground ginger
¼ teaspoon grated nutmeg
TO DECORATE:
150 ml/¼ pint whipping cream
ground cinnamon

1 Make the pastry. Place the flour in a bowl. Add the butter and rub in with the fingertips until the mixture resembles fine breadcrumbs. Stir in the sugar then add enough cold water, about 3-4 tablespoons, to mix to a firm dough.
2 Turn the dough out on to a lightly floured surface and knead briefly. Roll out and line a 23 cm/9 inch pie plate. Gather up the trimmings, reroll thinly and cut into leaf shapes. Brush the edge of the pie lightly with water and attach the leaves.

3 Make the filling. Mix the pumpkin purée, eggs, cream, sugar and spices in a large bowl. Pour into the pastry case and bake in a preheated oven, 190°C (375°F), Gas Mark 5 for 45-50 minutes, until the filling has set. Leave to cool.
4 To decorate the pie, whip the cream in a bowl until stiff. Spoon cream swirls around the rim of the pie and sprinkle with a little ground cinnamon.

Serves 6-8
Preparation time: 25 minutes
Cooking time: 45-50 minutes
Oven temperature: 190°C (375°F), Gas Mark 5

Autumn Fruit Cobbler

500 g/1 lb plums, halved
2 pears, chopped
250 g/8 oz blackberries
50 g/2 oz light muscovado sugar
COBBLER:
250 g/8 oz self raising flour
50 g/2 oz caster sugar
50 g/2 oz butter, diced
7-8 tablespoons milk
milk, for brushing
poppy seeds, for sprinkling

1 Mix all the fruit together in a bowl and turn into a buttered 1.2 litre/ 2 pint ovenproof dish.
2 Mix together the flour and sugar. Add the butter and rub in with the fingertips until the mixture resembles fine breadcrumbs. Stir in the milk and mix to a soft dough.
3 Roll out the dough to a 20 cm/ 8 inch square. Cut into 3 each way to make 9 squares. Arrange these over the fruit, brush with milk and sprinkle with poppy seeds.
4 Bake the cobbler in a preheated oven, 200°C (400°F), Gas Mark 6 for about 25-30 minutes, until the topping is golden brown. Serve hot with cream or custard.

Serves 6-8
Preparation time: 20 minutes
Cooking time: 25-30 minutes
Oven temperature: 200°C (400°F), Gas Mark 6

Pear and Blueberry Pie

This is a rough-and-ready pie in which the pastry does not quite meet the filling on top, giving a rustic charm.

PASTRY:
250 g/8 oz plain flour
125 g/4 oz chilled butter, diced
25 g/1 oz caster sugar
1 egg yolk
1 egg white, lightly beaten, to glaze
caster sugar, for dredging

FILLING:
4 firm pears, peeled, cored and
   chopped
500 g/1 lb blueberries
25 g/1 oz butter
50 g/2 oz light muscovado sugar

1 Make the pastry. Place the flour in a bowl. Add the butter and rub in with the fingertips until the mixture resembles fine breadcrumbs. Stir in the sugar, then add the egg yolk and enough cold water, about 3-4 tablespoons, to mix to a firm dough.

2 Turn the dough out on to a lightly floured surface and knead briefly. Roll out to a rough round about 35 cm/14 inches across. Lift the round on to a 23 cm/9 inch pie plate. Fill the centre of the pie with the pears and blueberries, dot with the butter and sprinkle with the muscovado sugar. Fold the overlapping pastry over the filling. Some of the filling will still show.

3 Brush the top of the pastry with egg white and dredge with caster sugar. Bake in a preheated oven, 200°C (400°F), Gas Mark 6 for 35-40 minutes until the pastry is golden brown. Serve warm.

Serves 6-8
Preparation time: 20 minutes
Cooking time: 35-40 minutes
Oven temperature: 200°C (400°F), Gas Mark 6

VARIATIONS

Old-Fashioned Rhubarb Pie

Omit the pears and blueberries and replace with 750 g/1½ lb sliced rhubarb. Bake as for the main recipe.

Old-Fashioned Apple Pie

Omit the pears and blueberries and replace with 750 g/1½ lb cooking apples, peeled, cored and sliced. Bake as for the main recipe.

Winter Fruit Pie

This deliciously fragrant pie is perfect for serving when supplies of fresh fruit are limited. The filling is even better when made the day before to allow the fruit to plump up.

PASTRY:

175 g/6 oz wholemeal self-raising flour
75 g/3 oz chilled butter, diced
25 g/1 oz caster sugar
beaten egg, to glaze

FILLING:

300 ml/½ pint red wine
1 strip of lemon rind
75 g/3 oz light muscovado sugar
1 cinnamon stick
pinch of grated nutmeg
175 g/6 oz ready-to-eat stoned prunes
175 g/6 oz ready-to-eat dried apricots
6 oranges, peeled and segmented

1 Make the filling. Warm the wine in a saucepan with the lemon rind, sugar and spices, stirring until the sugar has dissolved. Add the prunes and apricots, then simmer for 10 minutes, until slightly thickened.

2 Stir the oranges into the pan, then remove it from the heat. Remove the lemon rind and cinnamon stick.

3 Make the pastry. Place the flour in a bowl. Add the butter and rub in with the fingertips until the mixture resembles fine breadcrumbs. Stir in the sugar, then add enough cold water, about 3-4 tablespoons, to mix to a firm dough.

4 Turn the dough out on to a lightly floured surface and knead briefly. Spoon the filling into a 900 ml/ 1½ pint pie dish and brush the rim of the dish with water. Roll out the pastry to measure 5 cm/2 inches larger than the dish. Cut off a 2.5 cm/ 1 inch strip all round and press on to the rim of the pie dish.

5 Dampen the pastry edge lightly with water and cover the pie with the remaining pastry, trimming off the excess. Press the edges to seal, then pinch to decorate. Roll out the pastry trimmings and cut out leaf shapes, such as ivy and laurel. Attach these to the pie with a little water, then brush the pie with egg.

6 Bake the pie in a preheated oven, 200°C (400°F), Gas Mark 6 for 30-35 minutes, until the pastry is crisp and rich golden brown. Serve hot with cream or thick yogurt.

Serves 6
Preparation time: 35 minutes
Cooking time: 30-35 minutes
Oven temperature: 200°C (400°F), Gas Mark 6

Apple Crumble Pie

PASTRY:

175 g/6 oz self-raising flour

50 g/2 oz chilled butter, diced

25 g/1 oz caster sugar

1 egg, beaten

FILLING AND TOPPING:

500 g/1 lb cooking apples, peeled,
    cored and sliced

1 tablespoon lemon juice

75 g/3 oz plain flour

2 teaspoons ground cinnamon

50 g/2 oz chilled butter, diced

50 g/2 oz caster sugar

1 Make the pastry. Place the flour in a bowl, add the butter and rub in with the fingertips until the mixture resembles fine breadcrumbs. Stir in the sugar, then add the egg and a little water if necessary and mix to a soft dough.

2 Turn the dough out on a lightly floured surface and knead briefly. Roll out and line a 23 cm/9 inch flan tin. Mix the apples and lemon juice in a bowl and spread over the pastry case.

3 To make the crumble topping, mix the flour and cinnamon in a bowl.

Add the butter and rub in with the fingertips until the mixture resembles fine breadcrumbs. Stir in the sugar. Sprinkle over the apples.

4 Bake the pie in a preheated oven, 180°C (350°F), Gas Mark 4 for 40-45 minutes, until the topping is golden and the apples tender. Serve the pie warm.

Serves 6

Preparation time: 25 minutes

Cooking time: 40-45 minutes

Oven temperature: 180°C (350°F), Gas Mark 4

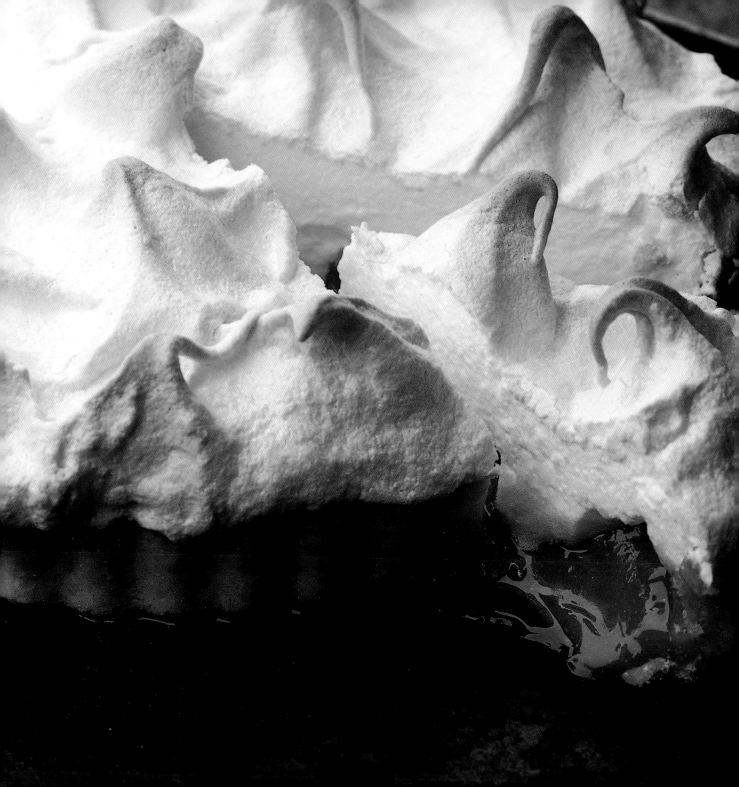

Butterscotch Meringue Pie

PASTRY:

125 g/4 oz plain flour
75 g/3 oz chilled butter, diced
25 g/1 oz caster sugar
50 g/2 oz ground hazelnuts
1 egg yolk

FILLING:

50 g/2 oz cornflour
125 g/4 oz dark muscovado sugar

300 ml/½ pint milk
50 g/2 oz butter, diced
3 egg yolks
1 teaspoon vanilla essence

MERINGUE:

3 egg whites
175 g/6 oz caster sugar

1 Make the pastry. Place the flour in a bowl, add the butter and rub in with the fingertips until the mixture resembles fine breadcrumbs. Stir in the sugar, ground hazelnuts and then add the egg yolk and enough cold water, about 2-3 tablespoons, to mix to a firm dough.
2 Knead the dough briefly on a lightly floured surface, then roll out and line a 20 cm/8 inch flan tin. Chill for 30 minutes, if time permits, then fill with crumpled foil and bake in a preheated oven, 200°C (400°F), Gas Mark 6 for 15 minutes. Remove the foil and bake the pastry case for a further 5 minutes.
3 Combine the cornflour and sugar in a saucepan. Blend in the milk until smooth. Heat gently, stirring until thickened, then cook for 1 minute. Cool the sauce slightly. Beat in the butter, a few pieces at a time, then stir in the egg yolks and vanilla. Pour the filling into the pastry case.
4 Whisk the egg whites in a grease-free bowl until they are stiff and dry. Whisk in 1 tablespoon of the sugar, then fold in the remainder. Spread the meringue over the filling to completely enclose it.
5 Return the pie to the oven for 10 minutes, until the meringue is golden. Serve warm or cold.

Serves 6
Preparation time: 35 minutes
Cooking time: 30 minutes
Oven temperature: 200°C (400°F), Gas Mark 6

VARIATION

Lemon Meringue Pie

PASTRY:

175 g/6 oz plain flour
75 g/3 oz chilled butter, cubed
25 g/1 oz caster sugar
50 g/2 oz ground hazelnuts
1 egg yolk

FILLING:

50 g/2 oz cornflour
125 g/4 oz caster sugar
300 ml/½ pint water
grated rind and juice of 2 lemons
3 egg yolks

MERINGUE:

3 egg whites
175 g/6 oz caster sugar

Make the pastry case as for the main recipe. To make the filling mix the cornflour and caster sugar in a saucepan. Stir in the water, lemon rind and juice until well blended. Bring to the boil, stirring until the sauce is thick and smooth. Cool slightly. Whisk the egg yolks in a bowl, then whisk in 2 tablespoons of the sauce. Return this mixture to the pan and cook gently until the sauce has thickened further. Pour the sauce into the pastry case. Make the meringue and bake as for the main recipe.

1 Mix the blackberries, sugar and lemon juice in a buttered 900 ml/1½ pint ovenproof dish.

2 Make the batter. Beat the egg and sugar in a bowl. Stir in the melted butter and milk. Sift the flour and cinnamon into the bowl and fold in lightly to form a smooth batter.

3 Pour the batter over the blackberries and bake in a preheated oven, 180°C (350°F), Gas Mark 4 for 25-30 minutes, until the topping is firm and blackberries tender. Serve warm.

Serves 4
Preparation time: 20 minutes
Cooking time: 25-30 minutes
Oven temperature: 180°C (350°F), Gas Mark 4

VARIATIONS

Blueberry Batter Pudding

Replace the blackberries with 500 g/1 lb blueberries and bake as for the main recipe.

Loganberry Batter Pudding

Replace the blackberries with 500 g/1 lb loganberries and bake as for the main recipe.

Blackberry Batter Pudding

This is a delicious dessert to make after a day's blackberry picking, or using fruit you gathered earlier and saved in the freezer.

500 g/1 lb blackberries
50 g/2 oz caster sugar
1 tablespoon lemon juice
BATTER:
1 egg
50 g/2 oz light muscovado sugar
50 g/2 oz butter, melted
4 tablespoons milk
125 g/4 oz self-raising flour
1 teaspoon ground cinnamon

Apricot and Almond Filo Pie

1 kg/2 lb apricots, halved and stoned
2 tablespoons lemon juice
50 g/2 oz blanched almonds, chopped
50 g/2 oz caster sugar
250 g/8 oz filo pastry, thawed if frozen
50 g/2 oz butter, melted
icing sugar, for dusting

1 Mix the apricots, lemon juice, almonds and caster sugar in a bowl.
2 Place 1 sheet of filo pastry over a greased 20 cm/8 inch flan tin. Brush with butter and place a second sheet on top of the first, at another angle. Continue layering the filo in this manner, with each successive sheet at a different angle, until only 2 sheets remain. Gently compress the filo sheets so that they take the shape of the tin, with the excess pastry sheets overlapping the tin.
3 Fill the pastry case with the apricot mixture, then layer the remaining 2 sheets of filo on top, brushing each with butter. Scrunch the overlapping edges of the pastry all round the top edge of the pie.
4 Brush the pie with any remaining butter and bake in a preheated oven, 190°C (375°F), Gas Mark 5 for 35-40 minutes, until the pastry is crisp and golden brown. Dust with icing sugar and serve warm or cold.

Serves 6
Preparation time: 20 minutes
Cooking time: 35-40 minutes
Oven temperature: 190°C (375°F), Gas Mark 5

VARIATION

Plum and Almond Pie

Replace the apricots with 1 kg/2 lb plums, halved and stoned and continue as in the main recipe.

SAVOURY PIES

Turkey, Spinach and Brie Filo Pie

175 g/6 oz frozen leaf spinach, thawed
75 g/3 oz butter
1 tablespoon olive oil
25 g/1 oz pine nuts
375 g/12 oz boneless turkey breast, cut into strips
175 g/6 oz Brie cheese, rind removed, cut into chunks
4 spring onions, chopped
1 teaspoon dried oregano
grated rind and juice of 1 lemon
250 g/8 oz frozen filo pastry, thawed
salt and pepper

1 Put the spinach in a colander. Press out the excess water, then chop roughly. Melt 25 g/1 oz of the butter with the oil in a pan. Add the pine nuts and brown. Add the turkey and fry until browned, lower the heat and fry for 5 minutes, until cooked. Transfer the contents of the pan to a bowl. Stir in the spinach, Brie, onions, oregano, lemon rind and juice. Season to taste and mix.
2 Grease a baking sheet and have ready the filo pastry, keeping the sheets of pastry covered while you work. Melt the remaining butter in a small pan.
3 Place 3 sheets of filo down the length of the baking sheet, overlapping each sheet by 2.5 cm/1 inch and brushing each with the melted butter (the pastry will overlap the baking sheet). Continue layering the sheets until you have 3 layers of pastry, brushing each layer with butter. Put the spinach filling on the centre third of the pastry to within 2.5 cm/1 inch of the top and bottom edges. Layer the remaining pastry sheets over the filling, brushing each with butter. Draw the top and bottom filo edges over, fold in both sides to enclose the filling, then scrunch the pastry on top.
4 Bake in a preheated oven, 200°C (400°F), Gas Mark 6 for 25 minutes, until the pastry is golden and crisp. Serve warm with a salad.

Serves 6-8
Preparation time: 25 minutes
Cooking time: 25 minutes
Oven temperature: 200°C (400°F), Gas Mark 6

Three Cheese Puff Pie

125 g/4 oz mozzarella cheese
175 g/6 oz Gorgonzola cheese
25 g/1 oz grated Parmesan
   cheese
25 g/1 oz pecan nuts, chopped
4 spring onions, chopped finely
2 tablespoons chopped fresh parsley
3 tablespoons crème fraîche
pepper
375 g/12 oz puff pastry, thawed
   if frozen
beaten egg, to glaze

1 Chop the mozzarella and Gorgonzola into pieces. Reserve 2 teaspoons of the Parmesan and mix the remainder with the other cheeses in a bowl. Add the pecans, spring onions, parsley and crème fraîche with pepper to taste. Mix.

2 Roll out half the pastry on a lightly floured surface to a 23 cm/9 inch square. Place on a greased baking sheet. Spread the cheese mixture over the top to within 1 cm/½ inch of the edges. Roll out the remaining pastry to a slightly larger square. Dampen the edges of the pastry with water and cover the pie. Press the edges together to seal and trim the edges if necessary. Flute the edge of the pie with the back of a sharp knife to form scallops.

3 Brush the top with the egg and sprinkle with the reserved Parmesan. Bake the pie in a preheated oven, 200°C (400°F), Gas Mark 6 for 25 minutes, until the pastry is risen and golden. Serve hot.

Serves 4-6
Preparation time: 20 minutes
Cooking time: 25 minutes
Oven temperature: 200°C (400°F), Gas Mark 6

Turkish Lamb and Apricot Pie

750 g/1½ lb boneless lamb, leg or fillet
½ teaspoon powdered saffron
1 teaspoon ground ginger
1 teaspoon ground cinnamon
1 teaspoon ground cumin
2 garlic cloves, crushed
1 onion, chopped finely
1 tablespoon olive oil
1 tablespoon clear honey
300 ml/½ pint water
125 g/4 oz ready-to-eat dried apricots, quartered
3 tablespoons chopped fresh parsley
salt and pepper

PASTRY:

25 g/1 oz sesame seeds
25 g/1 oz blanched almonds, finely chopped
200 g/7 oz plain flour
125 g/4 oz chilled butter, diced
beaten egg, to glaze

1 Place all the pie ingredients, except the parsley, in a large saucepan. Bring to the boil, skim off any scum with a slotted spoon, then stir well. Lower the heat and simmer, partly covered, for about 1 hour or until the lamb is tender. Stir in the parsley and leave to cool.

2 Make the pastry. Place the sesame seeds and almonds in a dry frying pan and heat gently until they are lightly toasted. Leave to cool.

3 Place the flour, with a little salt and pepper in a bowl. Add the butter and rub in with the fingertips until the mixture resembles fine breadcrumbs. Stir in the sesame seeds and almonds, then add enough water, about 3-4 tablespoons, to mix to a firm dough. Knead briefly on a lightly floured surface.

4 Turn the filling mixture into a 900 ml/1½ pint pie dish. Roll out the pastry to measure about 5 cm/ 2 inches larger all round than the pie dish. Cut off a 2.5 cm/1 inch strip all round and stick this to the rim of the pie dish with water. Moisten the strip with water. Cover the pie with the remaining pastry, pressing the edges well to seal.

5 Make a small hole in the top of the pie to allow the steam to escape. Brush the pastry with egg. Bake in a preheated oven, 200°C (400°F), Gas Mark 6 for 35 minutes, until the pastry is golden brown. Serve hot.

Serves 6
Preparation time: 1½ hours
Cooking time: 35 minutes
Oven temperature: 200°C (400°F), Gas Mark 6

Salmon in Puff Pastry

1 kg/2 lb salmon, skinned and filleted
25 g/1 oz butter
2 rindless streaky bacon rashers,
 chopped
125 g/4 oz mushrooms, chopped
125 g/4 oz soft cheese with garlic
 and herbs
2 tablespoons milk
500 g/1 lb puff pastry, thawed
 if frozen
beaten egg, to glaze
salt and pepper

1 Season the salmon fillets on both sides. Melt the butter in a frying pan, add the bacon and fry for about 5 minutes, until crisp. Add the mushrooms and fry for about 2 minutes, until softened, stirring all the time. Stir in the soft cheese and milk with salt and pepper to taste. Cook gently, stirring until well mixed. Remove from the heat and leave to cool.

2 Roll out half the pastry to measure 2.5 cm/1 inch larger all round than the reassembled fish. Transfer the pastry to a greased baking sheet and place one fish fillet, skinned side down, in the centre. Spread with the cheese mixture and cover with the second salmon fillet, skinned side up.

3 Brush the edges of the pastry with a little of the egg. Roll out the remaining pastry and cover the fish. Trim the edges, then pinch them together to seal. Roll out the pastry trimmings and cut them into strips. Brush the top of the pie with beaten egg and arrange the strips in a lattice design over the top. Brush again with beaten egg.

4 Bake the pie in a preheated oven, 200°C (400°F), Gas Mark 6 for 35-40 minutes, until the pastry is crisp and golden brown. Serve hot with asparagus or courgettes, or cold with a salad.

Serves 6-8
Preparation time: 30 minutes
Cooking time: 35-40 minutes
Oven temperature: 200°C (400°F), Gas Mark 6

VARIATION

Bass in Puff Pastry

1 kg/2 lb bass, skinned and filleted
1 bunch of watercress
25 g/1 oz butter, softened
1 garlic clove, chopped
1 tablespoon lemon juice
500 g/1 lb puff pastry, thawed
 if frozen
beaten egg, to glaze
salt and pepper

1 Season the bass fillets on both sides. Trim off any tough stalks from the watercress, wash and dry thoroughly. Plunge the watercress into a saucepan of salted, boiling water, cook for 1 minute, then drain and cool quickly under cold running water. Drain; dry well with paper towels, then chop the watercress finely.

2 Beat the butter, garlic and lemon juice in a bowl. Season to taste. Beat in the watercress. Continue from step 2 of the main recipe, substituting the watercress butter for the mushroom mixture. Bake as for the main recipe.

Spanakopita

Make the large version for supper or fill small filo parcels to serve with drinks.

1 kg/2 lb fresh spinach
2 tablespoons olive oil
1 onion, chopped
1 teaspoon dried oregano
250 g/8 oz feta cheese
4 eggs, beaten
grated nutmeg
375 g/12 oz filo pastry, thawed
    if frozen
50 g/2 oz butter, melted
salt and pepper

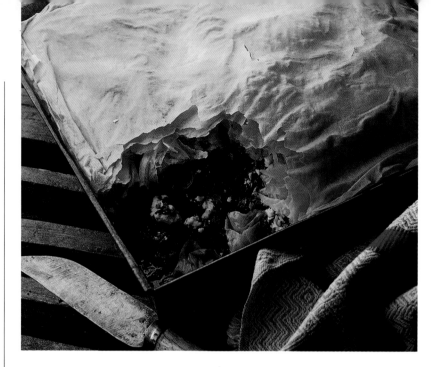

1 Wash the spinach in several changes of water, then place in a large saucepan with only the water that clings to the leaves. Cover and cook for 5-8 minutes, shaking the pan occasionally, until the spinach is tender. Drain well, pressing out as much water as possible, then chop the spinach finely and place in a large bowl.

2 Heat the oil in the clean saucepan, add the chopped onion and fry for about 5 minutes until softened. Add the contents of the pan to the spinach. Add the oregano. Crumble in the feta cheese, then stir in the eggs with nutmeg, salt and pepper to taste. Mix well.

3 Have ready a buttered shallow ovenproof dish, about 25 cm x 18 cm/10 x 7 inches in size. Layer the filo pastry in the dish, brushing each layer with butter and turning each successive sheet slightly to make angles all round. Continue until you have 3 sheets left.

4 Fill the pie with the spinach mixture. Fold over the edges of the filo pastry to cover the filling. Cover with the remaining filo sheets, tucking them in to fit the top of the dish, and brushing them with melted butter.

5 Bake the pie in a preheated oven, 190°C (375°F), Gas Mark 5 for 45-50 minutes, until the pastry is crisp and golden brown. Serve the pie hot or cold.

Serves 6
Preparation time: 30 minutes
Cooking time: 45-50 minutes
Oven temperature: 190°C (375°F), Gas Mark 5

VARIATION

Spanakopita Parcels

Make filling as before. Cut each filo sheet into 3 strips lengthways. Place a spoonful of filling along one short side, a little in from the edges. Brush with butter. Fold pastry sides over filling and roll up to enclose it. Place on a baking sheet. Continue making parcels until all the filling and pastry is used. Brush with butter and bake for 15-18 minutes, until golden. Serve warm or cold.

Makes about 60
Preparation time: 40 minutes
Cooking time: 15-18 minutes
Oven temperature: 190°C (375°F), Gas Mark 5

Leek and Ham Pie

50 g/2 oz butter

3 leeks, trimmed, cleaned and sliced

40 g/1½ oz plain flour

300 ml/½ pint milk

150 ml/¼ pint vegetable stock

175 g/6 oz thickly sliced cooked
   ham, chopped

salt and pepper

SCONE CRUST:

250 g/8 oz self-raising flour

50 g/2 oz chilled butter, diced

75 g/3 oz mature Cheddar cheese,
   grated

6-8 tablespoons milk

milk, to glaze

1 Melt the butter in a saucepan, add the leeks and fry gently until softened. Stir in the flour and cook for 1 minute. Gradually add the milk and vegetable stock, stirring until the sauce is thickened and smooth. Lower the heat and simmer for 5 minutes, then remove from the heat and stir in the chopped ham with salt and pepper to taste.

2 Make the scone crust. Place the flour in a bowl with a little salt and pepper. Add the butter and rub in until the mixture resembles fine breadcrumbs. Stir in the cheese, then add the milk and mix quickly to a soft dough.

3 Turn the leek mixture into a greased 1.2 litre/2 pint ovenproof dish. Press out the scone crust on a lightly floured surface to a round the same size as the dish. Cut into 8 wedges, then place on top of the pie. Brush with milk.

4 Bake the pie in a preheated oven, 200°C (400°F), Gas Mark 6 for 25-30 minutes, until the topping is golden brown. Serve hot.

Serves 4-6

Preparation time: 25 minutes

Cooking time: 25-30 minutes

Oven temperature: 200°C (400°F), Gas Mark 6

Ratatouille Pie

PASTRY:
175 g/6 oz plain flour
75 g/3 oz chilled butter, diced
25 g/1 oz grated Parmesan cheese
pinch of chilli powder
1 egg yolk
beaten egg or milk, to glaze
FILLING:
1 large aubergine
2 tablespoons olive oil
1 large onion, sliced thinly
2 garlic cloves, chopped
2 red peppers, cored, seeded
  and chopped
1 yellow pepper, cored, seeded
  and chopped
1 x 425 g/14 oz can chopped
  tomatoes
1 tablespoon tomato purée
1 tablespoon torn basil leaves
3 courgettes, sliced
salt and pepper

1 Make the filling. Cut the aubergine into cubes and place in a colander. Sprinkle with salt and leave for 30 minutes, to drain out any bitter juices. Rinse under cold running water, drain and dry well on paper towels.
2 Heat the oil in a large pan, add the onion and fry for 10 minutes, until softened. Stir in the garlic and peppers and fry for 5 minutes. Stir in the aubergine, tomatoes and tomato purée with salt and pepper to taste. Bring to the boil, lower the heat, cover and simmer for 20 minutes, then add the basil and courgettes and cook for 5 minutes more. Remove from the heat.
3 Make the pastry. Place the flour in a bowl, add the butter and rub in with the fingertips until the mixture resembles fine breadcrumbs. Stir in the Parmesan and chilli powder, then add the egg yolk and enough cold water, about 1-2 tablespoons, to mix to a firm dough.
4 Turn the dough out on a lightly floured surface and knead briefly. Roll out thinly and cut into 2.5 cm/1 inch wide strips with a knife or pastry wheel.
5 Turn the filling into a 1.2 litre/2 pint pie dish. Brush the rim of the dish with water and place a pastry strip all round, moisten with water. Arrange the pastry strips decoratively over the pie. Brush with egg or milk.
6 Bake the pie in a preheated oven, 200°C (400°F), Gas Mark 6 for 35-40 minutes, until the pastry is crisp and golden brown. Serve hot.

Serve 4-6
Preparation time: 1 hour
Cooking time: 35-40 minutes
Oven temperature: 200°C (400°F), Gas Mark 6

VARIATION

Chorizo, Aubergine and Tomato Pie

1 quantity pastry, see main recipe
FILLING:
500 g/1 lb aubergine
2 tablespoons olive oil
1 large onion, sliced thinly
175 g/6 oz chorizo sausage, sliced
2 garlic cloves, chopped
2 red peppers, cored, seeded
  and chopped
1 x 425 g/14 oz can chopped tomatoes
1 tablespoon tomato purée
salt and pepper

1 Cut the aubergine into cubes and place in a colander. Sprinkle with salt and leave for 30 minutes, to drain out any bitter juices. Rinse under cold running water, drain and dry well on paper towels.
2 Heat the oil in a large pan, add the onion and fry for 10 minutes, until softened and lightly browned. Stir in chorizo, garlic and peppers and fry for 5 minutes. Stir in the aubergine, tomatoes and tomato purée and season to taste. Bring to the boil, lower the heat, cover and simmer for 20 minutes, then remove from the heat.
3 Make and bake the pie from step 3 in the main recipe.

Chestnut, Celery and Mushroom Pie

PASTRY:

375 g/12 oz plain flour
1 teaspoon salt
75 g/3 oz butter or margarine
175 ml/6 fl oz water
beaten egg, to glaze

FILLING:

2 tablespoons olive oil
1 garlic clove, chopped
1 onion, chopped
1 carrot, chopped
3 celery sticks, chopped
1 x 425 g/14 oz can chestnuts, drained and chopped
250 g/8 oz chestnut mushrooms, chopped
150 ml/¼ pint vegetable stock
50 g/2 oz ground almonds
1 tablespoon chopped fresh herbs
2 eggs, beaten
salt and pepper

1 Make the filling. Heat the oil in a frying pan, add the garlic and onion and fry for about 5 minutes until softened. Add the carrot and celery and cook for 2-3 minutes, stirring occasionally. Stir in the chestnuts, mushrooms, stock, almonds and herbs with salt and pepper to taste. Bring to the boil, stirring until the mixture is heated through and well combined. Remove from the heat, cool slightly, then stir in the eggs. Leave to cool.

2 Make the pastry. Mix the flours and salt in a bowl. Melt the butter or margarine with the water in a saucepan. Add to the flour and mix quickly to a soft dough. Wrap closely and leave to rest at room temperature for 15 minutes.

3 Roll out two-thirds of the pastry on a lightly floured surface and line a greased loaf tin. Spread the chestnut mixture over the pastry case.

4 Roll out remaining pastry to a round large enough to cover the pie. Dampen the edges lightly with water and cover with the pastry lid. Trim the edges, reserving the trimmings. Pinch the edge of the pie to seal, then make a hole in the centre to allow the steam to escape.

5 Roll out the pastry trimmings and cut into leaves to decorate. Fix with a little egg, then brush the top of the pie all over with egg.

6 Bake in a preheated oven, 200°C (400°F), Gas Mark 6 for 40-50 minutes, until the pastry is crisp and golden. Cool the pie in the loaf tin for 10 minutes.. Carefully remove the pie from the tin and serve.

Serves 6
Preparation time: 30 minutes
Cooking time: 40-50 minutes
Oven temperature: 200°C (400°F), Gas Mark 6

Spiced Cauliflower Crumble Pie

2 tablespoons oil
1 onion, chopped
1 garlic clove, chopped
1 teaspoon chopped fresh root ginger
1 teaspoon cumin seeds
1 teaspoon mustard seeds
375 g/12 oz cauliflower, cut into
   small florets
1 tablespoon curry paste
1 x 425 g/14 oz can chopped tomatoes
1 x 425 g/14 oz can chick peas,
   drained
salt and pepper

CRUMBLE:

3 tablespoons olive oil
2 garlic cloves, chopped
50 g/2 oz fresh brown breadcrumbs
25 g/1 oz flaked almonds, toasted
2 tablespoons chopped fresh coriander
salt and pepper

1 Heat the oil in a frying pan, add the onion, garlic, ginger, cumin and mustard seeds and fry for about 5 minutes, until the onion is softened and lightly browned. Stir in the cauliflower and coat thoroughly in the spices.

2 Add the curry paste and tomatoes, with salt and pepper to taste. Bring to the boil, cover the pan and cook gently for 10-12 minutes or until the cauliflower is tender. Stir in the chick peas and heat through.

3 Make the crumble. Heat the oil in a saucepan, add the garlic and fry gently for about 2 minutes until softened. Stir in the breadcrumbs, flaked almonds and coriander with salt and pepper to taste. Mix well. Turn the vegetable mixture into a 900 ml/ 1½ pint ovenproof dish and sprinkle the crumble over the top.

4 Bake in a preheated oven, 200°C (400°F), Gas Mark 6 for 25 minutes, until the topping is crisp and golden brown. Serve hot.

Serves 4
Preparation time: 25 minutes
Cooking time: 25 minutes
Oven temperature: 200°C (400°F), Gas Mark 6

Steak and Kidney Pie

If it is helpful to do so, the meat mixture can be cooked the day before, ready to fill the pie.

750 g/1½ lb braising steak, cubed
250 g/8 oz ox kidney, cored
   and trimmed
1 large onion, chopped
1 celery stick, chopped
2 carrots, chopped
300 ml/½ pint water
½ teaspoon dried thyme

1 tablespoon soy sauce
1 tablespoon cornflour
2 tablespoons chopped fresh parsley
375 g/12 oz puff pastry, thawed
   if frozen
salt and pepper
beaten egg, to glaze

1 Combine the steak, kidney, onion, celery and carrots in a large saucepan. Add the water, thyme and soy sauce with salt and pepper to taste. Bring to the boil, then lower the heat, cover and simmer for about 1½ hours, until the meat is tender.

2 Taste and add more seasoning if necessary. In a cup, blend the cornflour to a paste with a little water. Stir into the pan, cooking until the meat sauce is thickened and smooth. Stir in the parsley and leave to cool.

3 Roll out half the pastry on a lightly floured surface and line a 1.2 litre/ 2 pint ovenproof dish or a 23 cm/9 inch pie plate. Place the cooled meat mixture over the pastry. Dampen the edges with water. Roll out the remaining pastry and cover the pie. Trim the edges, then cut up the edges with a knife and flute to seal and decorate.

4 Reroll the pastry trimmings and cut into leaves. Attach to the pie with a little of the beaten egg. Brush the top of the pie with more egg and bake in a preheated oven, 220°C (425°F), Gas Mark 7 for 35-40 minutes, until the pastry is crisp and golden brown. Serve hot with mashed potato and a green vegetable such as cabbage or Brussels sprouts.

Serves 6
Preparation time: 2 hours, plus cooling time
Cooking time: 35-40 minutes
Oven temperature: 220°C (425°F), Gas Mark 7

Chicken Pie

PASTRY:
250 g/8 oz plain flour
125 g/4 oz chilled butter, diced
beaten egg or milk, to glaze
1 tablespoon sesame seeds
FILLING:
1 tablespoon plain flour
4 skinless chicken portions, halved
25 g/1 oz butter
1 tablespoon olive oil
2 onions, chopped
300 ml/½ pint chicken stock
2 tablespoons lemon juice
150 ml/¼ pint double cream
1 bunch of parsley, chopped
salt and pepper

1 Make the pastry. Place the flour in a bowl, add the butter and rub in with the fingertips until the mixture resembles fine breadcrumbs. Add enough cold water, about 3-4 tablespoons, to mix to a firm dough.

2 Knead the dough on a lightly floured surface, then wrap closely and chill while preparing the filling.

3 Put the flour in a stout polythene bag and season. Add the chicken and toss until coated. Melt the butter and oil in a frying pan, add the onions and fry for 5 minutes until softened and browned. Remove the onions from the pan with a slotted spoon and set aside.

4 Add the chicken to the fat remaining in the pan and fry for

10 minutes, until browned. Using a slotted spoon, transfer the chicken to a 1.5 litre/2½ pint pie dish. Sprinkle the onions over the top.

5 Stir any remaining flour into the pan and cook for 1 minute. Gradually add the stock, stirring until the sauce is thick and smooth, scraping the base of the pan to incorporate any sediment. Stir in the lemon juice and bubble briefly. Stir in the cream and parsley and season to taste. Bring to the boil. Taste the sauce and adjust the seasoning, then pour it over the chicken.

6 Roll out the pastry to measure 5 cm/2 inches larger than the pie dish. Cut off a 2.5 cm/1 inch strip all round. Dampen the edge of the dish and attach the pastry strip. Brush the strip with water and cover the pie with the remaining pastry. Mark the edges of the top crust with a fork and make a hole in the centre to allow the steam to escape.

7 Brush with milk or beaten egg and sprinkle with sesame seeds. Bake in a preheated oven, 200°C (400°F), Gas Mark 6 for 30 minutes, then reduce to 180°C (350°F), Gas Mark 4 and bake for a further 45 minutes. Cover with foil if it becomes too brown. Serve hot.

Serves 4-6
Preparation time: 30 minutes
Cooking time: 1¼ hours
Oven temperature: 200°C (400°F), Gas Mark 6, then 180°C (350°F), Gas Mark 4

Camembert and Cranberry Pie

75 g/3 oz fresh or frozen cranberries
25 g/1 oz sugar
3 tablespoons water
1 tablespoon port
8 sheets filo pastry
25 g/1 oz butter, melted
1 whole Camembert cheese, about
   250 g/8 oz
pepper

1 Place the cranberries in a small saucepan with the sugar, water and port. Bring to the boil, then lower the heat and simmer gently until the cranberries pop and are just tender. This should take about 5 minutes. Leave to cool.

2 Layer the filo pastry on a greased baking sheet, brushing each layer with melted butter and arranging each one at a slightly different angle from the previous sheet to form points all round the edge. Place the Camembert in the centre and spread the cranberry sauce over the top. Season with pepper.

3 Gather up the filo pastry over the cheese and cranberry mixture, scrunching the edges together. Brush with the remaining butter.

4 Bake in a preheated oven, 200°C (400°F), Gas Mark 6 for 15-20 minutes, until it is golden. Cool on the baking sheet for 5 minutes, cut into wedges to serve.

Serves 4
Preparation time: 20 minutes
Cooking time: 15-20 minutes
Oven temperature: 200°C (400°F),
Gas Mark 6

Salmon and Red Pepper Pie

PASTRY:
375 g/12 oz plain flour
175 g/6 oz chilled butter, diced
2 egg yolks
salt and pepper
beaten egg or milk, to glaze

FILLING:
2 tablespoons olive oil
2 red peppers, cored, seeded
and chopped
2 eggs
250 g/8 oz salmon fillet, skinned
and cubed
1 courgette, sliced
1 teaspoon chopped fresh dill

1 Make the filling. Heat the oil in a saucepan. Add the peppers, with salt and pepper to taste. Cook gently for about 10 minutes, until softened. Purée in a blender or food processor. Alternatively, press the peppers through a sieve into a mixing bowl. Hard boil the eggs for 10 minutes, then drain, cool quickly and remove the shells.

2 Chop the eggs and add to the pepper purée with the salmon, courgette and dill. Mix well.

3 Make the pastry. Place the flour with ½ teaspoon salt in a bowl. Add the butter and rub in with the fingertips until the mixture resembles fine bread-crumbs. Add the egg yolks with enough cold water, about 3-4 tablespoons, to mix to a firm dough.

4 Turn the dough out on a lightly floured surface and knead briefly. Roll out just over half and line a 23 cm/9 inch pie plate. Fill with the salmon mixture and dampen the edges of the pastry with water.

5 Roll out the remaining pastry and cover the pie. Pinch the edges to seal, then crimp the edges to decorate. Reroll the pastry trimmings and cut them into fish tails or leaf shapes to decorate the pie. Attach the shapes with a little of the beaten egg or milk, then brush more egg or milk over the pie to glaze.

6 Bake the pie in a preheated oven, 200°C (400°F), Gas Mark 6 for 35-40 minutes, until the pastry is crisp and golden brown. Serve hot.

Serves 4-6
Preparation time: 25 minutes
Cooking time: 35-40 minutes
Oven temperature: 200°C (400°F), Gas Mark 6

Ham and Potato Pie

PASTRY:

175 g/6 oz plain flour
75 g/3 oz chilled butter, diced
50 g/2 oz mature Cheddar cheese, grated
milk or beaten egg, to glaze

FILLING:

2 tablespoons oil
1 onion, chopped
175 g/6 oz thickly sliced ham, chopped
50 g/2 oz sun-dried tomatoes, chopped
2 tablespoons chopped fresh parsley
3 tablespoons double cream
750 g/1½ lb floury potatoes, cooked and sliced thinly
salt and pepper

1 Place the flour in a large bowl, add the diced butter and rub in with the fingertips until the mixture resembles fine breadcrumbs. Stir in the grated cheese with a little salt and pepper, then add enough cold water, about 2-3 tablespoons, to make a firm dough.

2 Knead the dough briefly on a lightly floured surface, wrap closely and leave to rest while you prepare the filling.

3 Heat the oil in a frying pan, add the chopped onion and fry for about 5 minutes, until softened. Add the ham, sun-dried tomatoes, parsley and cream, with salt and pepper to taste. Bring to the boil, stirring until heated through.

4 Layer half the potatoes in a 1.5 litre/2 ½ pint pie dish and spread the ham mixture on top. Cover with the remaining potatoes. Roll out the pastry to measure 5 cm/2 inches larger than the pie dish. Cut off a 2.5 cm/1 inch strip all round and stick this to the rim of the pie dish with a little water.

5 Moisten the pastry strip with water, then cover the pie with the remaining pastry, pressing the edges to seal. Make a hole in the centre of the pie to allow the steam to escape. Brush the pastry with milk or egg and bake in a preheated oven, 200°C (400°F), Gas Mark 6 for 35 minutes, until the pastry is crisp and golden brown. Serve hot.

Serves 4-6
Preparation time: 30 minutes
Cooking time: 35 minutes
Oven temperature: 200°C (400°F), Gas Mark 6

Empanadas

These fried pastry turnovers are from Argentina, where they are eaten at every opportunity. They do freeze very well uncooked.

PASTRY:

250 g/8 oz plain flour
1 teaspoon paprika
50 g/2 oz butter
1 tablespoon oil
125 ml/4 fl oz water
oil, for deep frying

FILLING:

2 spring onions, chopped
1 tomato, chopped
50 g/2 oz cooked ham, chopped
50 g/2 oz Cheddar cheese, grated
1 x 200 g/7 oz can creamed sweetcorn
1 teaspoon chilli sauce
salt and pepper

1 Mix the flour and paprika with ½ teaspoon salt in a bowl. Heat the butter, oil and water in a pan until the butter has melted. Stir the mixture into the flour and mix to a soft dough. Turn out on to a lightly floured surface and knead briefly. Wrap closely and leave to rest at room temperature for 30 minutes.
2 Place all the filling ingredients in a bowl and mix well. Roll out the pastry thinly on a lightly floured surface. Cut into 12 x 10 cm/ 4 inch rounds using a pastry cutter. Place 2 teaspoons of filling on each round. Brush pastry edges with water and fold each round in half. Pinch the edges to seal and decorate.
3 Pour oil to a depth of about 2.5 cm/1 inch into a large frying pan. Heat the oil and fry the empanadas, a few at a time, for about 5 minutes, turning once, until evenly browned. Remove from the hot oil with a slotted spoon and drain on paper towels. Serve hot.

Makes 12
Preparation time: 30 minutes, plus resting time
Cooking time: 5-10 minutes

Crusty Shepherd's Pie

1 tablespoon olive oil
4 rindless smoked streaky bacon
    rashers, chopped
1 onion, chopped
500 g/1 lb minced lamb
1 teaspoon dried oregano
2 tablespoons chopped fresh parsley
150 ml/¼ pint red wine
425 g/14 oz canned or bottled passata
salt and pepper

SCONE TOPPING:
250 g/8 oz self-raising flour
50 g/2 oz chilled butter, diced
2 teaspoons wholegrain mustard
75 g/3 oz mature Cheddar cheese,
    grated
125 ml/4 fl oz milk

1 Heat the oil in a frying pan, add the bacon and onion and fry for about 5 minutes, until softened. Add the lamb and fry, stirring, until evenly browned.
2 Stir in the herbs, wine and passata with salt and pepper to taste. Bring to the boil, lower the heat and simmer, uncovered, for about 25 minutes, until the lamb is tender and the sauce thickened.
3 Make the scone topping. Place the flour in a bowl with salt and pepper. Add the butter and rub in with the fingertips until the mixture resembles fine breadcrumbs. Stir in the mustard and 50 g/2 oz of the cheese, then add enough of the milk to mix to a soft dough.
4 Knead the dough briefly on a lightly floured surface, then roll out to a thickness of 1 cm/½ inch. Stamp into 5 cm/2 inch scones. Reroll the trimmings and stamp out more rounds.
5 Transfer the meat mixture to a greased 1.2 litre/2 pint pie dish. Arrange the scones over the top, brush with milk and sprinkle with the remaining cheese. Bake in a preheated oven, 200°C (400°F), Gas Mark 6 for 25 minutes, until the topping is golden brown. Serve hot.

Serves 4-6
Preparation time: 40 minutes
Cooking time: 25 minutes
Oven temperature: 200°C (400°F), Gas Mark 6

VARIATIONS

Cheesy Shepherd's Pie

Omit the scone topping and replace it with 750 g/1½ lb cooked, mashed potato. Beat 25 g/1 oz butter and 3 tablespoons milk into the potato with salt and pepper to taste. Spread the topping over the pie. Sprinkle with 25 g/1 oz grated Cheddar cheese and bake as for the main recipe.

Scalloped Shepherd's Pie

Omit the scone topping and replace with 750 g/1½ lb sliced cooked potato. Cover the pie with overlapping slices of potato, and brush with 25 g/1 oz melted butter. Bake as for the main recipe.

Spiced Lentil Pie

PASTRY:

375 g/12 oz plain flour
175 g/6 oz butter or margarine, diced
2 teaspoons cumin seeds
2 teaspoons ground coriander
½ teaspoons chilli powder
3 tablespoons lemon juice

FILLING:

2 tablespoons sunflower oil
2 cloves garlic, crushed
1 onion, chopped
2 sticks celery, chopped
1 red pepper, seeded and chopped
125 g/4 oz red lentils
3 ripe tomatoes, skinned and chopped
¾ teaspoon chilli powder
450 ml/¾ pint vegetable stock
3 tablespoons chopped fresh coriander
2 tablespoons lemon juice
salt and pepper
beaten egg, to glaze

1 Measure the flour into a bowl. Add the butter and rub in with the fingertips until the mixture resembles breadcrumbs. Stir in the spices and salt, then add the lemon juice and 1-2 tablespoons of water and mix to a firm dough. Wrap closely and leave to rest at room temperature while preparing the filling.

2 Heat the oil, add the garlic and onion and fry for 5 minutes, until the onion is softened. Add the celery and red pepper and cook for a further 2 minutes. Stir in the lentils, tomatoes, chilli powder and stock and simmer uncovered, stirring occasionally for 25-30 minutes, until the lentils have absorbed the stock. Season to taste and stir in the coriander and lemon juice. Leave to cool.

3 Roll out just over half the pastry and line a 23 cm/9 inch pie plate. Spread over the filling and brush the pastry edges with water.

4 Roll out the remaining pastry and cover the pie. Pinch the edges together to seal. Brush the top with egg and bake in a preheated oven 200°C (400°F), Gas Mark 6 for 35-40 minutes, until golden brown. Cover the top with foil if it starts to over brown. Serve hot with a salad.

Serves 6
Preparation time: 40 minutes, plus cooling time
Cooking time: 35-40 minutes.
Oven temperature: 200°C (400°F), Gas Mark 6

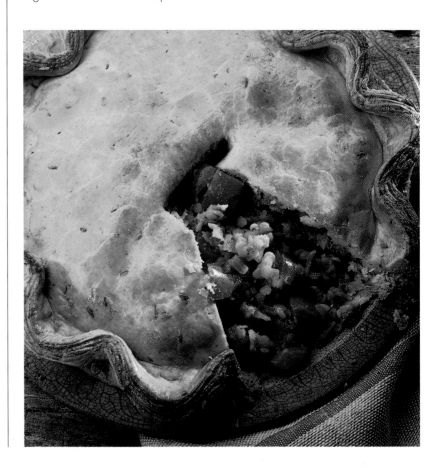

Scalloped Fish Pie

750 g/1½ lb haddock or cod fillet
2 bay leaves
6 peppercorns
450 ml/¾ pint milk
65 g/2½ oz butter
1 leek, trimmed, cleaned and sliced
40 g/1½ oz plain flour
2 tomatoes, skinned and quartered
2 tablespoons chopped fresh parsley
750 g/1½ lb potatoes, cooked and
   sliced thinly
salt and pepper

1 Place the fish in a frying pan with the bay leaves, peppercorns and milk. Add a little salt and pepper. Bring to the boil, then cover, lower the heat and simmer for about 10 minutes, until the fish is tender and flakes easily when tested with the tip of a knife. Using a slotted spoon, remove the fish from the pan; remove the skin and flake the flesh. Strain the cooking liquid into a jug.
2 Melt 40 g/1½ oz of the butter in a saucepan, add the sliced leek and fry for about 5 minutes until softened.

Stir in the plain flour and cook for 1 minute. Gradually add the milk, stirring until the sauce is thickened and smooth.
3 Remove the pan from the heat and stir in the fish, tomatoes and parsley with salt and pepper to taste. Melt the remaining butter in a small saucepan. Turn the fish mixture into a greased 1.2 litre/2 pint ovenproof dish. Arrange the potatoes over the top in overlapping rows. Brush with the butter.
4 Bake the pie in a preheated oven 200°C (400°F), Gas Mark 6 for 25 minutes, until the topping is golden brown. Serve hot with mange tout.

Serves 4
Preparation time: 25 minutes
Cooking time: 25 minutes
Oven temperature: 200°C (400°F),
Gas Mark 6

VARIATION

Smoked Haddock and Prawn Pie

Replace the white fish with 750 g/ 1½ lb smoked haddock and add 125 g/4 oz peeled cooked prawns, thawed if frozen, to the sauce. Cook as for the main recipe.

Game Pie

1 kg/2 lb prepared mixed game, such
   as venison, hare, rabbit or pheasant
500 g/1 lb herby sausages, skinned
175 g/6 oz smoked streaky bacon
4 tablespoons chopped fresh parsley
150 ml/¼ pint chicken or game stock
150 ml/¼ pint dry white wine
2 teaspoons powdered gelatine
salt and pepper

MARINADE:

150 ml/¼ pint red wine
2 bay leaves

4 juniper berries, bruised
1 onion, sliced
1 garlic clove, sliced
few sprigs of thyme
2 tablespoons olive oil
1 teaspoon sugar

PASTRY:

375 g/12 oz plain flour
½ teaspoon salt
75 g/3 oz lard or white fat
150 ml/¼ pint milk and water mixed
beaten egg, to glaze

1 Cut the meat into strips and place in a bowl. Add the marinade ingredients and mix. Cover and refrigerate overnight. The next day, remove the meat and dry. Discard the marinade. Break the sausages into pieces and mix with the game. Derind the bacon and chop, add with the parsley, season to taste.

2 Make the pastry, mix the flour and salt in a bowl. Melt the lard in the liquid in a pan, bring to the boil, then stir into the flour to form a soft dough. Wrap closely and leave to rest at room temperature for 30 minutes.

3 Remove two-thirds of the dough and roll out on a floured surface to line a greased 23 cm/9 inch long game pie tin. Check the pastry is even and pinch together any cracks. The pastry should overlap the top of the tin.

4 Pack the filling into the tin, pressing into the corners. Roll out the remaining pastry, dampen the edges and cover with pastry lid. Pinch edges to seal and decorate. Make a hole in the centre of the pie and push a foil funnel into it.

5 Roll out the pastry trimmings and use to decorate the pie. Stick on with the egg, use more egg to glaze the rest of the pie. Bake in a preheated oven, 200°C (400°F), Gas Mark 6 for 1 hour, then reduce to 180°C (350°F), Gas Mark 4 and bake for 1½ hours. If the crust browns too fast, cover with foil. Cool, then carefully remove from the tin. Boil the stock and wine in a pan for 5 minutes, then sprinkle the gelatine over and stir to dissolve. Cool until it starts to set, then pour into the pie through the funnel. Chill, then serve.

Serves 8-10
Preparation time: 45 minutes, plus marinating
Cooking time: 2½ hours
Oven temperature: 200°C (400°F), Gas Mark 6, then 180°C (350°F), Gas Mark 4

VARIATION

Turkey, Cranberry and Chestnut Pie

If you do not have a game pie tin then use a 1 kg/2 lb loaf tin.

1 quantity pastry, see main recipe
750 g/1½ lb turkey meat, cubed
250 g/8 oz sausagemeat
250 g/8 oz rindless streaky bacon, chopped
1 x 425 g/14 oz can chestnuts, drained and chopped
125 g/4 oz fresh or frozen cranberries
3 tablespoons chopped fresh parsley
1 teaspoon dried marjoram
1 egg beaten
150 ml/¼ pint turkey or chicken stock
1 teaspoon powdered gelatine

1 Combine the turkey, sausage-meat, bacon and chestnuts in a bowl. Season to taste and mix until evenly combined. Mix in the cranberries, herbs and egg.

2 Proceed as in the main recipe, filling the pie with the cubed turkey mixture and substituting turkey or chicken stock for the stock and wine mixture. A smaller quantity of liquid and gelatine is required for this pie because the cranberries create a moist filling.

3 Proceed and bake as in the main recipe.

Calzone

*Calzone are very simply rounds
of pizza dough folded over to
enclose a filling. Anything you
would put on a pizza can go
into a calzone, but this filling is
particularly flavoursome.
Calzone freeze well uncooked, so
make double the quantity and
stash half away for later.*

250 g/8 oz strong white flour
½ teaspoon salt
1 teaspoon easy-blend dried yeast
1 tablespoon olive oil
150 ml/¼ pint warm water
FILLING:
2 red peppers
2 tablespoons olive oil, plus extra
　for brushing
2 garlic cloves, chopped
50 g/2 oz sun-dried tomatoes, chopped
125 g/4 oz mozzarella cheese, cubed
2 slices of prosciutto, cut in strips
1 tablespoon grated Parmesan cheese
salt and pepper

1 Mix the flour, salt and yeast in a
bowl. Stir in the oil and warm water
and mix to a soft dough. Turn out on
to a lightly floured surface and knead
for 5 minutes. Place the dough in an
oiled polythene bag, tie it loosely
and leave to rise for 30 minutes.
2 Cut the peppers into quarters and
remove the seeds. Place under a
preheated hot grill, skin side up, for
about 10 minutes, until the skin is
charred. When cool enough to
handle, strip off the skins and cut the
pepper flesh into slices.
3 Heat the oil in a frying pan, add
the garlic and fry until lightly
browned. Remove from the heat and
stir in the peppers, sun-dried
tomatoes, cheese and prosciutto with
salt and pepper to taste.
4 Divide the dough in half. Roll out
each piece on a lightly floured
surface to a 25 cm/10 inch round.
Pile the filling on to one half of each
round, brush the edges with water
and fold the dough rounds in half.
Place the calzone on a greased
baking sheet, brush with a little olive
oil and sprinkle with the Parmesan.
5 Bake the calzone in a preheated
oven, 200°C (400°F), Gas Mark
6 for 20-25 minutes, until risen and
golden brown. Serve hot.

Makes 2
Preparation time: 25 minutes, plus
rising time
Cooking time: 20-25 minutes
Oven temperature: 200°C (400°F),
Gas Mark 6

Pork and Cider Pie with Potato Pastry

PASTRY:
75 g/3 oz butter
6 spring onions, chopped
175 g/6 oz plain flour
125 g/4 oz mashed potato
milk, to glaze
1 teaspoon mustard seeds
1 teaspoon poppy seeds
FILLING:
1 tablespoon plain flour
2 teaspoons paprika
750 g/1½ lb lean pork, such as
fillet, cubed
2 tablespoons oil
1 onion, chopped
450 ml/¾ pint dry cider
2 teaspoons wholegrain mustard
2 eating apples, peeled, cored
and sliced
3 tablespoons thick Greek yogurt
salt and pepper

1 Make the filling. Combine the flour and paprika in a stout polythene bag. Season with salt and pepper. Add the pork and toss it in the seasoned flour until evenly coated. Heat the oil in a large frying pan, add the onion and fry for about 5 minutes, until softened. Add the pork and fry until lightly browned. Stir in any leftover flour and cook for 1 minute.

2 Gradually stir in the cider, cooking until the mixture is thickened and smooth. Stir in the mustard, add the apple slices and bring to the boil. Lower the heat, cover and simmer for 40 minutes, until the pork is tender, then leave to cool.

3 Make the pastry. Melt 25 g/1 oz of the butter in a small saucepan, add the spring onions and fry until softened. Cool slightly.

4 Put the flour in a bowl. Cut the remaining butter into cubes and rub it into the flour until the mixture resembles fine breadcrumbs. Add the spring onions with the cooking juices, then stir in the mashed potato with salt and pepper to taste. Mix to a soft dough.

5 Stir the yogurt into the pork mixture; turn it into a 1.8 litre/3 pint pie dish. Dampen the rim of the dish with water. Roll out the pastry on a lightly floured surface to a size 5 cm/ 2 inches larger than the pie dish. Tuck the pastry under 2.5 cm/1 inch all round and cover the pie. Press the edges to seal. Brush the pastry with milk and sprinkle with mustard and poppy seeds.

6 Bake the pie in a preheated oven, 200°C (400°F), Gas Mark 6 for 30 minutes, until the pastry is crisp and golden brown. Serve hot with green beans or cabbage.

Serves 4-6
Preparation time: 1½ hours
Cooking time: 30 minutes
Oven temperature: 200°C (400°F), Gas Mark 6